UNIVERSITY CASEBOOK SERIES®

2021 SUPPLEMENT TO
CONSTITUTIONAL LAW
CASES AND MATERIALS
SIXTEENTH EDITION

JONATHAN D. VARAT
Professor of Law Emeritus and Former Dean
University of California, Los Angeles School of Law

VIKRAM D. AMAR
Dean and Iwan Foundation Professor of Law
University of Illinois College of Law

EVAN H. CAMINKER
Branch Rickey Collegiate Professor of Law and Former Dean
University of Michigan Law School

FOUNDATION
PRESS

University Casebook Series is a trademark registered in the U.S. Patent and Trademark Office.

© 2021 LEG, Inc. d/b/a West Academic
    444 Cedar Street, Suite 700
    St. Paul, MN 55101
    1-877-888-1330

Printed in the United States of America

ISBN: 978-1-64708-884-2

TABLE OF CONTENTS

TABLE OF CASES

The principal cases are in bold type.

UNIVERSITY CASEBOOK SERIES®

2021 SUPPLEMENT TO
CONSTITUTIONAL LAW
CASES AND MATERIALS
SIXTEENTH EDITION

PART 1

THE CONSTITUTION AND THE COURTS: THE JUDICIAL FUNCTION IN CONSTITUTIONAL CASES

CHAPTER 3

THE JURISDICTION OF FEDERAL COURTS IN CONSTITUTIONAL CASES

3. CASES AND CONTROVERSIES AND JUSTICIABILITY

B. STANDING

1. "CONVENTIONAL" STANDING

Page 74. Add after Village of Arlington Heights v. Metropolitan Housing Development Corp.:

California v. Texas

593 U.S. ___, 141 S.Ct. 2104 (2021).

In 2010, Congress enacted the Patient Protection and Affordable Care Act, 124 Stat. 119, which comprehensively regulated the health insurance industry and included an "individual mandate" that required most Americans to obtain "minimum essential" health insurance coverage. 26 U.S.C. § 5000A(a). The Act also imposed a monetary penalty, scaled according to income, upon individuals who failed to do so. A group of States and other plaintiffs sued to enjoin the Act's operation, arguing that Congress lacked the power to impose the individual mandate and that the mandate was not severable from the rest of the statute's many regulations, and so the entire Act must fall. In 2012, the Supreme Court held (in a 5–4 decision) that the individual mandate exceeded Congress's Commerce Clause power but was a valid exercise of Congress's taxing power. See National Federation of Independent Business v. Sebelius, 567 U.S. 519 (2012).[a] In 2017, Congress effectively nullified the penalty for non-purchase, amending the Act to set the penalty amount to $0. Tax Cuts and Jobs Act of 2017, 131 Stat. 2092, 26 U.S.C. § 5000A(c). Post-amendment IRS rules made clear that the statute no longer requires taxpayers to report whether they maintain the insurance coverage prescribed in § 5000A(a). In 2018 Texas and 17 other States, later joined by two individuals, sued various federal officials claiming that the mandate can no longer be defended as a tax in the absence of financial consequences. Arguing that (according to *Sebelius*) Congress has no other power to impose it and repeating that the mandate is not severable from the rest of the Act, they sought an injunction against the Act's enforcement in its entirety.

The Court, in an opinion authored by Justice Breyer and joined by six others, held that the plaintiffs lacked standing to challenge the individual mandate, as "[n]either the individual nor the state plaintiffs have shown that the injury they will suffer or have suffered is 'fairly traceable' to the 'allegedly unlawful conduct' of which they complain."

The Court assumed the individual plaintiffs suffered a financial injury in fact through their purchase of the minimum essential insurance coverage prescribed by

---

[a]   For fuller treatment of those two holdings, see 16th edition text at pp. 183 and 202.

3

§ 5000A(a). But the Court held that this injury was not traceable to the mandate: the required Article III injury must be caused by actions of government officials rather than by unenforceable laws on the books. "Their problem lies in the fact that the statutory provision, while it tells them to obtain that coverage, has no means of enforcement. With the penalty zeroed out, the IRS can no longer seek a penalty from those who fail to comply. . . . Because of this, there is no possible Government action that is causally connected to the plaintiffs' injury—the costs of purchasing health insurance. Or to put the matter conversely, that injury is not 'fairly traceable' to any 'allegedly unlawful conduct' of which the plaintiffs complain. Allen v. Wright, 468 U. S. 737, 751 (1984). They have not pointed to any way in which the defendants, the Commissioner of Internal Revenue and the Secretary of Health and Human Services, will act to enforce § 5000A(a). They have not shown how any other federal employees could do so either. In a word, they have not shown that any kind of Government action or conduct has caused or will cause the injury they attribute to § 5000A(a)." The Court continued: "[O]ur cases have consistently spoken of the need to assert an injury that is the result of a statute's actual or threatened *enforcement*, whether today or in the future."

The Article III requirement of redressability also "makes clear that the statutory language alone is not sufficient. To determine whether an injury is redressable, a court will consider the relationship between 'the judicial relief requested' and the 'injury' suffered. *Allen*, 468 U. S., at 753, n. 19. The plaintiffs here sought injunctive relief and a declaratory judgment. The injunctive relief, however, concerned the Act's other provisions that they say are inseverable from the minimum essential coverage requirement. The relief they sought in respect to the only provision they attack as unconstitutional—the minimum essential coverage provision—is declaratory relief, namely, a judicial statement that the provision they attacked is unconstitutional. . . . Remedies, however, ordinarily 'operate with respect to specific parties.' . . . In the absence of any specific party, they do not simply operate 'on legal rules in the abstract.' "

The Court observed that "[t]he matter is not simply technical. To find standing here to attack an unenforceable statutory provision would allow a federal court to issue what would amount to 'an advisory opinion without the possibility of any judicial relief.' . . . It would threaten to grant unelected judges a general authority to conduct oversight of decisions of the elected branches of Government. . . ."

With respect to the state plaintiffs, the Court held that they "have similarly failed to show that they have alleged an 'injury fairly traceable to the defendant's allegedly *unlawful* conduct.' " The States claimed "two kinds of pocketbook injuries." First, they claimed that the individual mandate has led state residents to enroll in various state-operated or state-sponsored insurance programs, for which the states must pay a share of the new enrollees' costs. But "the States also have failed to show how this injury is directly traceable to any actual or possible unlawful Government conduct in enforcing § 5000A(a). . . . That alone is enough to show that they, like the individual plaintiffs, lack Article III standing."

The Court observed another "fatal weakness" of causation: the state plaintiffs failed to show that the individual mandate, without any prospect of penalty, will lead more individuals to enroll in the cost-sharing state programs. "We have said that, where a causal relation between injury and challenged action depends upon the decision of an independent third party (here an individual's decision to enroll in, say, Medicaid), 'standing is not precluded, but it is ordinarily "substantially more difficult" to establish' . . . . To satisfy that burden, the plaintiff must show at the least 'that third parties will likely react in predictable ways.' . . ." But here, "the programs to which the state plaintiffs point offer their recipients many benefits that have nothing to do with the minimum essential coverage provision of § 5000A(a). . . . Given these benefits, neither logic nor intuition suggests that the presence of the [mandate] would lead an individual to enroll in one of those programs that its absence would lead them to ignore. A penalty might have led some inertia-bound individuals to enroll. But without a penalty, what incentive could the provision provide?" The Court concluded: "Unsurprisingly, the States have not demonstrated that an unenforceable mandate will cause their residents to enroll in valuable benefits programs that they would otherwise forgo. It would require far stronger evidence than the States have offered here to support their counterintuitive theory of standing, which rests on a 'highly attenuated chain of possibilities.' "

Second, the state plaintiffs also claimed to suffer additional pocketbook injuries: costs of providing information to beneficiaries of state health plans about their health insurance coverage and costs of providing related information to the IRS. "The problem with these claims, however, is that other provisions of [the] Act, not the minimum essential coverage provision, impose these other requirements. Nothing in the text of these form provisions suggests that they would not operate without § 5000A(a). . . . To show that the minimum essential coverage requirement is unconstitutional would not show that enforcement of any of these other provisions violates the Constitution. The state plaintiffs do not claim the contrary. The Government's conduct in question is therefore not 'fairly traceable' to enforcement of the 'allegedly unlawful' provision of which the plaintiffs complain—§ 5000A(a). *Allen*, 468 U. S., at 751." For the same reason, the Court dismissed other asserted pocketbook injuries linked to other expenditure-inducing provisions of the Act.

Justice Alito, joined by Justice Gorsuch, dissented. He argued that "[t]he States have clearly shown that they suffer concrete and particularized financial injuries that are traceable to the conduct of the Federal Government." The dissent did not claim these injuries were directly traceable to the challenged individual mandate *per se*. Rather, the dissent's theory of traceability "proceeds in two steps." The States argued first that the mandate is unconstitutional; and second that the cost-imposing provisions of the Act cannot be severed from the mandate. If both steps were accepted as alleged, then "it follows that the Government cannot lawfully enforce those obligations against the States." In other words, the dissent accepted a "standing-through-inseverability" theory: the assumption of inseverability creates the required Article III connection between the assertedly illegal conduct (the individual mandate) and the asserted injury (costs imposed by the Act's other provisions).[b]

The Court did not address the dissent's "novel alternative theory of standing," declining to consider it because it was not presented in either the lower courts or the petition for certiorari.[c]

---

[b]   Reaching the merits, the dissent would have declared the individual mandate unconstitutional, found the mandate inseverable from the provisions imposing costs on the state plaintiffs, and enjoined enforcement of each of these challenged injury-causing provisions.

[c]   Justice Thomas concurred in the Court's opinion, writing separately that this alternative theory "offers a connection between harm and unlawful conduct" and "might well support standing in some circumstances, as it has some support in history and our case law." But he agreed with the Court that this standing-through-inseverability argument was not properly addressed here.

For a deeper dive into the standing-through-inseverability theory, see Vikram Amar, Caminker, & Mazzone, *"Standing" In Unfamiliar Territory: Part Two in a Series on the California v. Texas Affordable Care Act Case*, justia.com, https://verdict.justia.com/2020/10/13/standing-in-unfamiliar-territory-part-two-in-a-series-on-the-california-v-texas-affordable-care-act-case (2020).

Page 76. Add after Gill v. Whitford:

Carney v. Adams, 593 U.S. ___, 141 S.Ct. 493 (2021). The Delaware Constitution's political-balance requirements for several major courts dictate that no more than a bare majority of judges "shall be of the same political party" and the other judges "shall be of the other major political party," so only Democrats or Republicans may serve as judges on these courts. Adams, a registered independent, claimed these requirements violated his First Amendment right of freedom of association. The Court held that Adams lacked standing because, based on the record at summary judgment, he was not "able and ready" to apply for a judicial vacancy and therefore lacked a concrete, particularized, and imminent injury. The Court refused to credit Adams' claim that he wanted to apply to become a judge on one of these courts: his statement of intent "stand[s] alone without any actual past injury, without reference to an anticipated timeframe, without prior judgeship applications, without prior relevant conversations, without efforts to determine likely openings, without other preparations or investigations, and without any other supporting evidence." The Court noted that Adams, within a matter of weeks, had read a law review article arguing the exclusion of independent-party judges is unconstitutional; switched his party affiliation from Democrat to independent; and then filed suit. These circumstances all "suggest[ ] an abstract, generalized grievance, not an actual desire to become a judge."

Uzuegbunam v. Preczewski, 593 U.S. ___, 141 S.Ct. 792 (2021). A college's free speech zone policy prohibited speech that "disturbs the peace and/or comfort of person(s)." After being stopped from speaking based on listeners' complaints, a student sued various college officials charged with enforcing the speech policy for violating his First Amendment rights. The college discontinued the policy, rendering the student's claim for injunctive relief moot. The Court held that the student still had standing to seek nominal damages, however, because they would serve to redress his completed First Amendment violation. The Court based this characterization of nominal damages on history: the prevailing rule at common law permitted a party whose rights were invaded to recover nominal damages without furnishing evidence of actual damage. Rather than purely symbolic, nominal damages were considered the default remedy unless and until the plaintiff showed she was entitled to some other form of damages. So while "a single dollar often cannot provide full redress," even a partial remedy constituted redress under the common law and thus nominal damages satisfy the redressability element of modern standing requirements. Chief Justice Roberts' lone dissent, complaining that "federal courts will be required to give advisory opinions whenever a plaintiff tacks on a request for a dollar," argued in response that at least the defendant should be able to fully moot the claim for nominal damages by "fork[ing] over a buck" so that this claim would not itself require a court to reach the merits.

2.   TAXPAYER AND CITIZEN STANDING

Citizen Standing

Page 84. Add after Spokeo, Inc. v. Robins:

TransUnion LLC v. Ramirez

593 U.S. ___, 141 S.Ct. 2190, ___ L.Ed.2d ___ (2021).

■ JUSTICE KAVANAUGH delivered the opinion of the Court.

To have Article III standing to sue in federal court, plaintiffs must demonstrate, among other things, that they suffered a concrete harm. No concrete harm, no standing. Central to assessing concreteness is whether the asserted harm has a "close relationship" to a harm traditionally recognized as providing a basis for a lawsuit in American courts—such as physical harm, monetary harm, or various intangible harms including (as relevant here) reputational harm. Spokeo, Inc. v. Robins, 578 U. S. 330, 340–341 (2016).

In this case, a class of 8,185 individuals sued TransUnion, a credit reporting agency, in federal court under the Fair Credit Reporting Act. The plaintiffs claimed that TransUnion failed to use reasonable procedures to ensure the accuracy of their credit files, as maintained internally by TransUnion. For 1,853 of the class members, TransUnion provided misleading credit reports to third-party businesses. We conclude that those 1,853 class members have demonstrated concrete reputational harm and thus have Article III standing to sue on the reasonable-procedures claim. The internal credit files of the other 6,332 class members were *not* provided to third-party businesses during the relevant time period. We conclude that those 6,332 class members have not demonstrated concrete harm and thus lack Article III standing to sue on the reasonable-procedures claim.

In two other claims, all 8,185 class members complained about formatting defects in certain mailings sent to them by TransUnion. But the class members other than the named plaintiff Sergio Ramirez have not demonstrated that the alleged formatting errors caused them any concrete harm. Therefore, except for Ramirez, the class members do not have standing as to those two claims.

Over Judge McKeown's dissent, the U. S. Court of Appeals for the Ninth Circuit ruled that all 8,185 class members have standing as to all three claims. The Court of Appeals approved a class damages award of about $40 million. In light of our conclusion that (i) only 1,853 class members have standing for the reasonable-procedures claim and (ii) only Ramirez himself has standing for the two formatting claims relating to the mailings, we reverse the judgment of the Ninth Circuit and remand the case for further proceedings consistent with this opinion.

I

[In 1970, Congress passed the Fair Credit Reporting Act. 84 Stat. 1127, as amended, 15 U.S.C. § 1681 *et seq.* In order to promote "fair and accurate credit reporting" and to protect consumer privacy, the Act regulates the consumer reporting agencies that compile and disseminate personal information about consumers. Three requirements are relevant here. First, consumer reporting agencies must "follow reasonable procedures to assure maximum possible accuracy" in consumer reports. § 1681e(b). Second, the agencies must, upon request, disclose to the consumer "[a]ll information in the consumer's file at the time of the request." § 1681g(a)(1). Third, the agencies must "provide to a consumer, with each written disclosure by the agency to the consumer," a "summary of rights" prepared by the Consumer Financial Protection Bureau (CFPB). § 1681g(c)(2). The Act creates a cause of action for injured consumers: "Any person who willfully fails to comply with any requirement imposed under this subchapter with respect to any consumer is liable to that consumer" for actual damages or for statutory damages not less than $100 and not more than $1,000, as well as for punitive damages and attorney's fees. § 1681n(a).

[TransUnion, one of the "Big Three" credit reporting agencies, compiles personal and financial information about individual consumers to create consumer reports, which it then sells to entities such as banks, landlords, and car dealerships that request information about consumers' creditworthiness. Beginning in 2002, TransUnion introduced an add-on product called OFAC Name Screen Alert. OFAC, the U. S. Treasury Department's Office of Foreign Assets Control, maintains a list of "specially designated nationals" who threaten America's national security (such as terrorists, drug traffickers, or other serious criminals), with whom it is generally unlawful to transact business. When a business requested OFAC in addition to other consumer information, TransUnion used third-party software to compare the consumer's name against the OFAC list. If the consumer's first and last name matched the first and last name of an individual on OFAC's list, then TransUnion would place an alert on the credit report indicating that the consumer's name was a "potential match." TransUnion did not compare any data other than first and last names (for example, middle names, initials, or birth dates). Unsurprisingly, TransUnion's process generated many false positives, as thousands of law-abiding Americans share a first and last name with one of the terrorists, drug traffickers, or serious criminals on OFAC's list.

[In 2011, Sergio Ramirez tried to purchase a car but was refused when the dealer obtained his credit report through TransUnion and learned that Ramirez matched a name on the OFAC database. Ramirez called TransUnion to request a copy of his credit file; he received a mailing that included his file and the statutorily required summary of rights prepared by the CFPB but did not mention the OFAC alert. TransUnion then mailed Ramirez a second letter alerting him that his name was considered a potential match to names on the OFAC list, but this second mailing did not include an additional copy of the summary of rights. TransUnion eventually removed the OFAC alert from Ramirez's file.

[In February 2012, Ramirez sued TransUnion and alleged three violations of the Fair Credit Reporting Act: TransUnion (1) failed to follow reasonable procedures to ensure the accuracy of information in his credit file; (2) failed to provide him with all of the information in his credit file upon his request; and (3) failed to provide him with a summary of his rights "with each written disclosure," because TransUnion's second mailing did not contain a summary of his rights. The district court certified a class of all people in the United States to whom TransUnion sent a mailing similar in form to Ramirez's second mailing during the period from January 1, 2011, to July 26, 2011. The parties stipulated that the class contained 8,185 members, of which only 1,853 members (including Ramirez) had their credit reports disseminated by TransUnion to potential creditors during the same time period. The district court ruled that all 8,185 class members had Article III standing to assert all three claims, and after trial the jury awarded the plaintiffs more than $60 million in statutory and punitive damages. The U. S. Court of Appeals for the Ninth Circuit affirmed in relevant part (though reducing the punitive damages award), over a dissent arguing that only the 1,853 class members whose reports were actually disseminated had standing to pursue the reasonable-procedures claim and only Ramirez had standing to pursue the two claims related to deficient mailings.]

. . .

II

The question in this case is whether the 8,185 class members have Article III standing as to their three claims. In Part II, we summarize the requirements of Article III standing—in particular, the requirement that plaintiffs demonstrate a "concrete harm." In Part III, we then apply the concrete-harm requirement to the plaintiffs' lawsuit against TransUnion.

A

. . . Article III confines the federal judicial power to the resolution of "Cases" and "Controversies." For there to be a case or controversy under Article III, the plaintiff must have a " 'personal stake' " in the case—in other words, standing. . . . To demonstrate their personal stake, plaintiffs must be able to sufficiently answer the question: " 'What's it to you?' " Scalia, The Doctrine of Standing as an Essential Element of the Separation of Powers, 17 Suffolk U. L. Rev. 881, 882 (1983).

To answer that question in a way sufficient to establish standing, a plaintiff must show (i) that he suffered an injury in fact that is concrete, particularized, and actual or imminent; (ii) that the injury was likely caused by the defendant; and (iii) that the injury would likely be redressed by judicial relief. Lujan v. Defenders of Wildlife, 504 U. S. 555, 560–561 (1992). If "the plaintiff does not claim to have suffered an injury that the defendant caused and the court can remedy, there is no case or controversy for the federal court to resolve." . . .

Requiring a plaintiff to demonstrate a concrete and particularized injury caused by the defendant and redressable by the court ensures that federal courts decide only "the rights of individuals," Marbury v. Madison, 1 Cranch 137, 170 (1803), and that federal courts exercise "their proper function in a limited and separated government," Roberts, Article III Limits on Statutory Standing, 42 Duke L. J. 1219, 1224 (1993). Under Article III, federal courts do not adjudicate hypothetical or abstract disputes. . . .

B

The question in this case focuses on the Article III requirement that the plaintiff's injury in fact be "concrete"—that is, "real, and not abstract." Spokeo, Inc. v. Robins, 578 U. S. 330, 340 (2016) . . . . What makes a harm concrete for purposes of Article III? As a general matter, the Court has explained that "history and tradition offer a meaningful guide to the types of cases that Article III empowers federal courts to consider." . . . And with respect to the concrete-harm requirement in particular, this Court's opinion in Spokeo v. Robins indicated that courts should assess whether the alleged injury to the plaintiff has a "close relationship" to a harm "traditionally" recognized as providing a basis for a lawsuit in American courts. 578 U. S., at 341. That inquiry asks whether plaintiffs have identified a close historical or common-law analogue for their asserted injury. *Spokeo* does not require an exact duplicate in American history and tradition. But *Spokeo* is not an open-ended invitation for federal courts to loosen Article III based on contemporary, evolving beliefs about what kinds of suits should be heard in federal courts.

As *Spokeo* explained, certain harms readily qualify as concrete injuries under Article III. The most obvious are traditional tangible harms, such as physical harms and monetary harms. If a defendant has caused physical or monetary injury to the plaintiff, the plaintiff has suffered a concrete injury in fact under Article III.

Various intangible harms can also be concrete. Chief among them are injuries with a close relationship to harms traditionally recognized as providing a basis for lawsuits in American courts. *Id.*, at 340–341. Those include, for example, reputational harms, disclosure of private information, and intrusion upon seclusion.... And those traditional harms may also include harms specified by the Constitution itself. See, *e.g.*, *Spokeo*, 578 U. S., at 340 . . . (abridgment of free speech), and Church of Lukumi Babalu Aye, Inc. v. Hialeah, 508 U. S. 520 (1993) (infringement of free exercise)).

In determining whether a harm is sufficiently concrete to qualify as an injury in fact, the Court in *Spokeo* said that Congress's views may be "instructive." 578 U. S., at 341. Courts must afford due respect to Congress's decision to impose a statutory prohibition or obligation on a defendant, and to grant a plaintiff a cause of action to sue over the defendant's violation of that statutory prohibition or obligation. See *id.*, at 340–341. In that way, Congress may "elevate to the status of legally cognizable injuries concrete, *de facto* injuries that were previously inadequate in law." *Id.*, at 341 . . . . But even though "Congress may 'elevate' harms that 'exist' in the real world before Congress recognized them to actionable legal status, it may not simply enact an injury into existence, using its lawmaking power to transform something that is not remotely harmful into something that is." . . . .

Importantly, this Court has rejected the proposition that "a plaintiff automatically satisfies the injury-in-fact requirement whenever a statute grants a person a statutory right and purports to authorize that person to sue to vindicate that right." *Spokeo*, 578 U. S., at 341. As the Court emphasized in *Spokeo*, "Article III standing requires a concrete injury even in the context of a statutory violation." *Ibid.*

. . .

For standing purposes, therefore, an important difference exists between (i) a plaintiff's statutory cause of action to sue a defendant over the defendant's violation of federal law, and (ii) a plaintiff's suffering concrete harm because of the defendant's violation of federal law. Congress may enact legal prohibitions and obligations. And Congress may create causes of action for plaintiffs to sue defendants who violate those legal prohibitions or obligations. But under Article III, an injury in law is not an injury in fact. Only those plaintiffs who have been *concretely harmed* by a defendant's statutory violation may sue that private defendant over that violation in federal court. . . .[1]

. . .

A regime where Congress could freely authorize *unharmed* plaintiffs to sue defendants who violate federal law not only would violate Article III but also would infringe on the Executive Branch's Article II authority. We accept the "displacement of

---

[1]   The lead dissent [authored by Justice Thomas] notes that the terminology of injury in fact became prevalent only in the latter half of the 20th century. That is unsurprising because until the 20th century, Congress did not often afford federal "citizen suit"-style causes of action to private plaintiffs who did not suffer concrete harms. For example, until the 20th century, Congress generally did not create "citizen suit" causes of action for private plaintiffs to sue the Government. . . . Moreover, until Abbott Laboratories v. Gardner, 387 U. S. 136 (1967), a plaintiff often could not bring a pre-enforcement suit against a Government agency or official under the Administrative Procedure Act arguing that an agency rule was unlawful; instead, a party could raise such an argument only in an enforcement action. Likewise, until the 20th century, Congress rarely created "citizen suit"-style causes of action for suits against private parties by private plaintiffs who had not suffered a concrete harm. All told, until the 20th century, this Court had little reason to emphasize the injury-in-fact requirement because, until the 20th century, there were relatively few instances where litigants without concrete injuries had a cause of action to sue in federal court. The situation has changed markedly, especially over the last 50 years or so. During that time, Congress has created many novel and expansive causes of action that in turn have required greater judicial focus on the requirements of Article III. See, *e.g.*, Spokeo, Inc. v. Robins, 578 U. S. 330 (2016); . . . . Lujan v. Defenders of Wildlife, 504 U. S. 555 (1992).

the democratically elected branches when necessary to decide an actual case." Roberts, 42 Duke L. J., at 1230. But otherwise, the choice of how to prioritize and how aggressively to pursue legal actions against defendants who violate the law falls within the discretion of the Executive Branch, not within the purview of private plaintiffs (and their attorneys). Private plaintiffs are not accountable to the people and are not charged with pursuing the public interest in enforcing a defendant's general compliance with regulatory law. See *Lujan*, 504 U. S., at 577.

In sum, the concrete-harm requirement is essential to the Constitution's separation of powers. To be sure, the concrete-harm requirement can be difficult to apply in some cases. Some advocate that the concrete-harm requirement be ditched altogether, on the theory that it would be more efficient or convenient to simply say that a statutory violation and a cause of action suffice to afford a plaintiff standing. But as the Court has often stated, "the fact that a given law or procedure is efficient, convenient, and useful in facilitating functions of government, standing alone, will not save it if it is contrary to the Constitution." . . . So it is here.[3]

III

We now apply those fundamental standing principles to this lawsuit. . . .

. . .

A

We first address the plaintiffs' claim that TransUnion failed to "follow reasonable procedures to assure maximum possible accuracy" of the plaintiffs' credit files maintained by TransUnion. . . . In particular, the plaintiffs argue that TransUnion did not do enough to ensure that OFAC alerts labeling them as potential terrorists were not included in their credit files.

Assuming that the plaintiffs are correct that TransUnion violated its obligations under the Fair Credit Reporting Act to use reasonable procedures in internally maintaining the credit files, we must determine whether the 8,185 class members suffered concrete harm from TransUnion's failure to employ reasonable procedures.

1

Start with the 1,853 class members (including the named plaintiff Ramirez) whose reports were disseminated to third-party businesses. The plaintiffs argue that the publication to a third party of a credit report bearing a misleading OFAC alert injures the subject of the report. The plaintiffs contend that this injury bears a "close relationship" to a harm traditionally recognized as providing a basis for a lawsuit in

---

[3] [Justice Thomas's] lead dissent would reject the core standing principle that a plaintiff must always have suffered a concrete harm, and would cast aside decades of precedent articulating that requirement, such as *Spokeo* [and] *Lujan*. . . . As we see it, the dissent's theory would largely outsource Article III to Congress. As we understand the dissent's theory, a suit seeking to enforce "general compliance with regulatory law" would not suffice for Article III standing because such a suit seeks to vindicate a duty owed to the whole community. . . . But under the dissent's theory, so long as Congress frames a defendant's obligation to comply with regulatory law as an obligation owed to *individuals,* any suit to vindicate that obligation suddenly suffices for Article III. Suppose, for example, that Congress passes a law purporting to give all American citizens an individual right to clean air and clean water, as well as a cause of action to sue and recover $100 in damages from any business that violates any pollution law anywhere in the United States. The dissent apparently would find standing in such a case. We respectfully disagree. In our view, unharmed plaintiffs who seek to sue under such a law are still doing no more than enforcing general compliance with regulatory law. And under Article III and this Court's precedents, Congress may not authorize plaintiffs who have not suffered concrete harms to sue in federal court simply to enforce general compliance with regulatory law.

American courts—namely, the reputational harm associated with the tort of defamation. Spokeo, Inc. v. Robins, 578 U. S. 330, 341 (2016).

We agree with the plaintiffs. Under longstanding American law, a person is injured when a defamatory statement "that would subject him to hatred, contempt, or ridicule" is published to a third party. . . . TransUnion provided third parties with credit reports containing OFAC alerts that labeled the class members as potential terrorists, drug traffickers, or serious criminals. The 1,853 class members therefore suffered a harm with a "close relationship" to the harm associated with the tort of defamation. We have no trouble concluding that the 1,853 class members suffered a concrete harm that qualifies as an injury in fact.

. . .

2

The remaining 6,332 class members are a different story [because] TransUnion did not provide those plaintiffs' credit information to any potential creditors during the class period from January 2011 to July 2011. Given the absence of dissemination, we must determine whether the 6,332 class members suffered some other concrete harm for purposes of Article III.

. . .

[The answer is no, as] there is "no historical or common-law analog where the mere existence of inaccurate information, absent dissemination, amounts to concrete injury." . . . "Since the basis of the action for words was the loss of credit or fame, and not the insult, it was always necessary to show a publication of the words."

. . . The mere presence of an inaccuracy in an internal credit file, if it is not disclosed to a third party, causes no concrete harm. In cases such as these where allegedly inaccurate or misleading information sits in a company database, the plaintiffs' harm is roughly the same, legally speaking, as if someone wrote a defamatory letter and then stored it in her desk drawer. A letter that is not sent does not harm anyone, no matter how insulting the letter is. So too here.

Because the plaintiffs cannot demonstrate that the misleading information in the internal credit files itself constitutes a concrete harm, the plaintiffs advance a separate argument based on an asserted *risk of future harm*. They say that the 6,332 class members suffered a concrete injury for Article III purposes because the existence of misleading OFAC alerts in their internal credit files exposed them to a material risk that the information would be disseminated in the future to third parties and thereby cause them harm. The plaintiffs rely on language from *Spokeo* where the Court said that "the risk of real harm" (or as the Court otherwise stated, a "material risk of harm") can sometimes "satisfy the requirement of concreteness." 578 U. S., at 341–342 (citing Clapper v. Amnesty Int'l USA, 568 U. S. 398 (2013)).

. . . But importantly, *Clapper* involved a suit for *injunctive relief* . . . [and] a plaintiff's standing to seek injunctive relief does not necessarily mean that the plaintiff has standing to seek retrospective damages.

TransUnion advances a persuasive argument that in a suit for damages, the mere risk of future harm, standing alone, cannot qualify as a concrete harm—at least unless the exposure to the risk of future harm itself causes a *separate* concrete harm. . . .[7]

---

[7] For example, a plaintiff's knowledge that he or she is exposed to a risk of future physical, monetary, or reputational harm could cause its own current emotional or psychological harm. We take no position on whether or how such an emotional or psychological harm could suffice for Article III

TransUnion contends that if an individual is exposed to a risk of future harm, time will eventually reveal whether the risk materializes in the form of actual harm. If the risk of future harm materializes and the individual suffers a concrete harm, then the harm itself, and not the pre-existing risk, will constitute a basis for the person's injury and for damages. If the risk of future harm does *not* materialize, then the individual cannot establish a concrete harm sufficient for standing, according to TransUnion.

. . .

Here, the 6,332 plaintiffs did not demonstrate that the risk of future harm materialized—that is, that the inaccurate OFAC alerts in their internal TransUnion credit files were ever provided to third parties or caused a denial of credit. Nor did those plaintiffs present evidence that the class members were independently harmed by their exposure to the risk itself—that is, that they suffered some other injury (such as an emotional injury) from the mere risk that their credit reports would be provided to third-party businesses. Therefore, the 6,332 plaintiffs' argument for standing for their damages claims based on an asserted risk of future harm is unavailing.

Even apart from that fundamental problem with their argument based on the risk of future harm . . . the risk of dissemination to third parties . . . was too speculative to support Article III standing. . . . The plaintiffs claimed that TransUnion could have divulged their misleading credit information to a third party at any moment. But the plaintiffs did not demonstrate a sufficient likelihood that their individual credit information would be requested by third-party businesses and provided by TransUnion during the relevant time period. Nor did the plaintiffs demonstrate that there was a sufficient likelihood that TransUnion would otherwise intentionally or accidentally release their information to third parties. "Because no evidence in the record establishes a serious likelihood of disclosure, we cannot simply presume a material risk of concrete harm." . . .

Moreover, the plaintiffs did not present any evidence that the 6,332 class members even *knew* that there were OFAC alerts in their internal TransUnion credit files. If those plaintiffs prevailed in this case, many of them would first learn that they were "injured" when they received a check compensating them for their supposed "injury." It is difficult to see how a risk of future harm could supply the basis for a plaintiff's standing when the plaintiff did not even know that there was a risk of future harm.

. . .

B

We next address the plaintiffs' standing to recover damages for two other claims in the complaint: the disclosure claim and the summary-of-rights claim. Those two claims are intertwined.

In the disclosure claim, the plaintiffs alleged that TransUnion breached its obligation to provide them with their complete credit files upon request. According to the plaintiffs, TransUnion sent the plaintiffs copies of their credit files that omitted the OFAC information, and then in a second mailing sent the OFAC information. . . . In the summary-of-rights claim, the plaintiffs further asserted that TransUnion should have included another summary of rights in that second mailing—the mailing that included the OFAC information. . . . As the plaintiffs note, the disclosure and summary-of-rights

---

purposes—for example, by analogy to the tort of intentional infliction of emotional distress. . . . The plaintiffs here have not relied on such a theory of Article III harm. They have not claimed an emotional distress injury from the risk that a misleading credit report might be sent to a third-party business. Nor could they do so, given that the 6,332 plaintiffs have not established that they were even aware of the misleading information in the internal credit files maintained at TransUnion.

requirements are designed to protect consumers' interests in learning of any inaccuracies in their credit files so that they can promptly correct the files before they are disseminated to third parties.

In support of standing, the plaintiffs thus contend that the TransUnion mailings were formatted incorrectly and deprived them of their right to receive information in the format required by statute. But the plaintiffs have not demonstrated that the format of TransUnion's mailings caused them a harm with a close relationship to a harm traditionally recognized as providing a basis for a lawsuit in American courts. See *Spokeo*, 578 U. S., at 341. In fact, they do not demonstrate that they suffered any harm *at all* from the formatting violations. The plaintiffs presented no evidence that, other than Ramirez, "a single other class member so much as *opened* the dual mailings," "nor that they were confused, distressed, or relied on the information in any way." . . . The plaintiffs put forth no evidence, moreover, that the plaintiffs would have tried to correct their credit files—and thereby prevented dissemination of a misleading report—had they been sent the information in the proper format. . . . Without any evidence of harm caused by the format of the mailings, these are "bare procedural violation[s], divorced from any concrete harm." *Spokeo*, 578 U. S., at 341. That does not suffice for Article III standing.

. . .

For its part, the United States as *amicus curiae*, but not the plaintiffs, separately asserts that the plaintiffs suffered a concrete "informational injury" under several of this Court's precedents. See Federal Election Comm'n v. Akins, 524 U. S. 11 (1998) . . . . We disagree. The plaintiffs did not allege that they failed to receive any required information. They argued only that they received it *in the wrong format*. Therefore, *Akins* [does] not control here. In addition, those cases involved denial of information subject to public-disclosure or sunshine laws that entitle all members of the public to certain information. This case does not involve such a public-disclosure law. . . . Moreover, the plaintiffs have identified no "downstream consequences" from failing to receive the required information. . . . They did not demonstrate, for example, that the alleged information deficit hindered their ability to correct erroneous information before it was later sent to third parties. An "asserted informational injury that causes no adverse effects cannot satisfy Article III." . . .

* * *

No concrete harm, no standing. The 1,853 class members whose credit reports were provided to third-party businesses suffered a concrete harm and thus have standing as to the reasonable-procedures claim. The 6,332 class members whose credit reports were not provided to third-party businesses did not suffer a concrete harm and thus do not have standing as to the reasonable-procedures claim. As for the claims pertaining to the format of TransUnion's mailings, none of the 8,185 class members other than the named plaintiff Ramirez suffered a concrete harm.

We reverse the judgment of the U. S. Court of Appeals for the Ninth Circuit and remand the case for further proceedings consistent with this opinion. . . .

It is so ordered.

■ JUSTICE THOMAS, with whom JUSTICE BREYER, JUSTICE SOTOMAYOR, AND JUSTICE KAGAN join, dissenting.

TransUnion generated credit reports that erroneously flagged many law-abiding people as potential terrorists and drug traffickers. In doing so, TransUnion violated several provisions of the Fair Credit Reporting Act (FCRA) that entitle consumers to accuracy in credit-reporting procedures; to receive information in their credit files; and to receive a summary of their rights. Yet despite Congress' judgment that such misdeeds deserve redress, the majority decides that TransUnion's actions are so insignificant that the Constitution prohibits consumers from vindicating their rights in federal court. The Constitution does no such thing.

. . .

II

A

. . .

. . . Article III "does not extend the judicial power to every violation of the constitution" or federal law "which may possibly take place." . . . Rather, the power extends only "to 'a case in law or equity,' in which a *right*, under such law, is asserted." . . .

Key to the scope of the judicial power, then, is whether an individual asserts his or her own rights. At the time of the founding, whether a court possessed judicial power over an action with no showing of actual damages depended on whether the plaintiff sought to enforce a right held privately by an individual or a duty owed broadly to the community. See Spokeo, Inc. v. Robins, 578 U. S. 330, 344–346 (2016) (Thomas, J., concurring) . . . . Where an individual sought to sue someone for a violation of his private rights, such as trespass on his land, the plaintiff needed only to allege the violation. . . . Courts typically did not require any showing of actual damage. See Uzuegbunam v. Preczewski, 592 U. S.___, ___ (2021). But where an individual sued based on the violation of a duty owed broadly to the whole community, such as the overgrazing of public lands, courts required "not only *injuria* [legal injury] but also *damnum* [damage]." *Spokeo*, 578 U. S., at 346 (Thomas, J., concurring) . . . .

This distinction mattered not only for traditional common-law rights, but also for newly created statutory ones. The First Congress enacted a law defining copyrights and gave copyright holders the right to sue infringing persons in order to recover statutory damages, even if the holder "could not show monetary loss." . . . In the patent context, a defendant challenged an infringement suit brought under a similar law. Along the lines of what TransUnion argues here, the infringer contended that "the making of a machine cannot be an offence, because no action lies, except for actual damage, and there can be no actual damages, or even a rule for damages, for an infringement by making a machine." . . . Riding circuit, Justice Story rejected that theory, noting that the plaintiff could sue in federal court merely by alleging a violation of a private right: "[W]here the law gives an action for a particular act, the doing of that act imports of itself a damage to the party" because "[e]very violation of a right imports some damage." . . .[2]

The principle that the violation of an individual right gives rise to an actionable harm was widespread at the founding, in early American history, and in many modern cases. See *Uzuegbunam*, 592 U. S., at ___ (collecting cases); Havens Realty Corp. v. Coleman, 455 U. S. 363, 373 (1982) ("[T]he actual or threatened injury required by Art. III may exist solely by virtue of statutes creating legal rights, the invasion of which creates standing" . . . .) And this understanding accords proper respect for the power of Congress and other legislatures to define legal rights. No one could seriously dispute,

---

[2]   The "public rights" terminology has been used to refer to two different concepts. . . . Here, in contrast, the term "public rights" refers to duties owed collectively to the community. For example, Congress owes a duty to all Americans to legislate within its constitutional confines. But not every single American can sue over Congress' failure to do so. Only individuals who, at a minimum, establish harm beyond the mere violation of that constitutional duty can sue. . . .

for example, that a violation of property rights is actionable, but as a general matter, "[p]roperty rights are created by the State." Palazzolo v. Rhode Island, 533 U. S. 606, 626 (2001). In light of this history, tradition, and common practice, our test should be clear: So long as a "statute fixes a minimum of recovery . . ., there would seem to be no doubt of the right of one who establishes a technical ground of action to recover this minimum sum without any specific showing of loss." T. Cooley, Law of Torts *271. While the Court today discusses the supposed failure to show "injury in fact," courts for centuries held that injury in law to a private right was enough to create a case or controversy.

B

Here, each class member established a violation of his or her private rights. The jury found that TransUnion violated three separate duties created by statute. . . . All three of those duties are owed to individuals, not to the community writ large. . . .

Were there any doubt that consumer reporting agencies owe these duties to specific individuals—and not to the larger community—Congress created a cause of action providing that "[a]ny person who willfully fails to comply" with an FCRA requirement "with respect to any *consumer* is liable to *that consumer*." § 1681n(a) (emphasis added). If a consumer reporting agency breaches any FCRA duty owed to a specific consumer, then that individual (not all consumers) may sue the agency. No one disputes that each class member possesses this cause of action. And no one disputes that the jury found that TransUnion violated each class member's individual rights. The plaintiffs thus have a sufficient injury to sue in federal court.

C

The Court chooses a different approach. Rejecting this history, the majority holds that the mere violation of a personal legal right is *not*—and never can be—an injury sufficient to establish standing. What matters for the Court is only that the "injury in fact be 'concrete.' " "No concrete harm, no standing."

That may be a pithy catchphrase, but it is worth pausing to ask why "concrete" injury in fact should be the sole inquiry. After all, it was not until 1970—"180 years after the ratification of Article III"—that this Court even introduced the "injury in fact" (as opposed to injury in law) concept of standing. . . . And the concept then was not even about constitutional standing; it concerned a *statutory* cause of action under the Administrative Procedure Act. . . .

The Court later took this statutory requirement and began to graft it onto its constitutional standing analysis. See, *e.g.,* Warth v. Seldin, 422 U. S. 490 (1975). But even then, injury in fact served as an *additional* way to get into federal court. Article III injury still could "exist solely by virtue of 'statutes creating legal rights, the invasion of which creates standing.' " *Id.,* at 500 . . . . So the introduction of an injury-in-fact requirement, in effect, "represented a substantial broadening of access to the federal courts." Simon v. Eastern Ky. Welfare Rights Organization, 426 U. S. 26, 39 (1976). A plaintiff could now invoke a federal court's judicial power by establishing injury by virtue of a violated legal right *or* by alleging some *other* type of "personal interest." *Ibid.*

In the context of public rights, the Court continued to require more than just a legal violation. In Lujan v. Defenders of Wildlife, 504 U. S. 555 (1992), for example, the Court concluded that several environmental organizations lacked standing to challenge a regulation about interagency communications, even though the organizations invoked a citizen-suit provision allowing " 'any person [to] commence a civil suit . . . to enjoin any person . . . who is alleged to be in violation of' " the law. . . . Echoing the historical distinction between duties owed to individuals and those owed to the community, the

Court explained that a plaintiff must do more than raise "a generally available grievance about government—claiming only harm to his and every citizen's interest in proper application of the Constitution and laws." 504 U. S., at 573. "Vindicating the *public* interest (including the public interest in Government observance of the Constitution and laws) is the function of Congress and the Chief Executive." *Id.,* at 576. " 'The province of the court,' " in contrast, " 'is, solely, to decide on the rights of individuals.' " *Ibid.* (quoting Marbury v. Madison, 1 Cranch 137, 170 (1803)).

. . .

In *Spokeo*, the Court built on this approach. Based on a few sentences from *Lujan* . . . the Court concluded that a plaintiff does not automatically "satisf[y] the injury-in-fact requirement whenever a statute grants a person a statutory right and purports to authorize that person to sue to vindicate that right." *Spokeo*, 578 U. S., at 341. But the Court made clear that "Congress is well positioned to identify intangible harms that meet minimum Article III requirements" and explained that "the violation of a procedural right granted by statute *can be* sufficient in some circumstances to constitute injury in fact." *Id.,* at 341, 342 (emphasis added).

Reconciling these statements has proved to be a challenge. . . . But "[t]he historical restrictions on standing" offer considerable guidance. . . . A statute that creates a public right plus a citizen-suit cause of action is insufficient by itself to establish standing. See *Lujan*, 504 U. S., at 576.[4] A statute that creates a private right and a cause of action, however, *does* gives plaintiffs an adequate interest in vindicating their private rights in federal court. . . .

The majority today, however, takes the road less traveled: "[U]nder Article III, an injury in law is not an injury in fact." . . . No matter if the right is personal or if the legislature deems the right worthy of legal protection, legislatures are constitutionally unable to offer the protection of the federal courts for anything other than money, bodily integrity, and anything else that this Court thinks looks close enough to rights existing at common law. The 1970s injury-in-fact theory has now displaced the traditional gateway into federal courts.

This approach is remarkable in both its novelty and effects. Never before has this Court declared that legal injury is *inherently* insufficient to support standing.[5] And never before has this Court declared that legislatures are constitutionally precluded from creating legal rights enforceable in federal court if those rights deviate too far from their common-law roots. According to the majority, courts alone have the power to sift and weigh harms to decide whether they merit the Federal Judiciary's attention. In the name of protecting the separation of powers, this Court has relieved the legislature of its power to create and define rights.

---

[4] But see Caminker, Comment, The Constitutionality of *Qui Tam* Actions, 99 Yale L. J. 341, 342, n. 3 (1989) ("Six statutes [enacted by the First Congress] imposed penalties and/or forfeitures for conduct injurious to the general public and expressly authorized suits by private informers, with the recovery being shared between the informer and the United States"); McCulloch v. Maryland, 4 Wheat. 316, 317, 321–322 (1819) (reviewing "an action of debt brought by the defendant in error . . . who sued as well for himself as for the State of Maryland . . . to recover certain penalties").

[5] See, *e.g.,* Lujan v. Defenders of Wildlife, 504 U. S. 555, 578 (1992) ("Nothing in this contradicts the principle that the injury required by Art. III may exist solely by virtue of 'statutes creating legal rights, the invasion of which creates standing" . . .); Warth v. Seldin, 422 U. S. 490, 514 (1975) ("Congress may create a statutory right or entitlement the alleged deprivation of which can confer standing to sue even where the plaintiff would have suffered no judicially cognizable injury in the absence of statute*")*; Linda R. S. v. Richard D., 410 U. S. 614, 617, n. 3 (1973) ("Congress may enact statutes creating legal rights, the invasion of which creates standing, even though no injury would exist without the statute").

III

Even assuming that this Court should be in the business of second-guessing private rights, this is a rather odd case to say that Congress went too far. TransUnion's misconduct here is exactly the sort of thing that has long merited legal redress.

As an initial matter, this Court has recognized that the unlawful withholding of requested information causes "a sufficiently distinct injury to provide standing to sue." Public Citizen v. Department of Justice, 491 U. S. 440, 449 (1989); see also *Havens Realty Corp.*, 455 U. S., at 374. Here, TransUnion unlawfully withheld from each class member the OFAC version of his or her credit report that the class member requested. And TransUnion unlawfully failed to send a summary of rights. The majority's response is to contend that the plaintiffs actually did not allege that they failed to receive any required information; they alleged only that they received it in the *"wrong format."*

That reframing finds little support in the complaint . . . [and] also finds no footing in the record. . . .

Were there any doubt about the facts below, we have the helpful benefit of a jury verdict. . . .

. . .

And then there is the standalone harm caused by the rather extreme errors in the credit reports. The majority (rightly) decides that having one's identity falsely and publically associated with terrorism and drug trafficking is itself a concrete harm. For good reason. This case is a particularly grave example of the harm this Court identified as central to the FCRA: "curb[ing] the dissemination of false information." *Spokeo*, 578 U.S., at 342. And it aligns closely with a "harm that has traditionally been regarded as providing a basis for a lawsuit." *Id.*, at 341. . . .

The question this Court has identified as key, then, is whether a plaintiff established "a degree of risk" that is "sufficient to meet the concreteness requirement." *Spokeo,* 578 U. S., at 343. Here, in a 7-month period, it is undisputed that nearly 25 percent of the class had false OFAC-flags sent to potential creditors. . . . If 25 percent is insufficient, then, pray tell, what percentage is?

The majority deflects this line of analysis by all but eliminating the risk-of-harm analysis. According to the majority, an elevated risk of harm simply shows that a concrete harm is *imminent* and thus may support only a claim for injunctive relief. But this reworking of *Spokeo* fails for two reasons. First, it ignores what *Spokeo* said: "[Our opinion] does not mean . . . that the risk of real harm cannot satisfy the requirement of concreteness." *Spokeo*, 578 U. S., at 341. Second, it ignores what *Spokeo* did. The Court in *Spokeo* remanded the respondent's claims for statutory damages to the Ninth Circuit to consider "whether the . . . violations alleged in this case entail a degree of risk sufficient to meet the concreteness requirement." *Id.*, at 342–343. The theory that risk of harm matters only for injunctive relief is thus squarely foreclosed by *Spokeo* itself.

. . .

But even setting aside everything already mentioned—the Constitution's text, history, precedent, financial harm, libel, the risk of publication, and actual disclosure to a third party—one need only tap into common sense to know that receiving a letter identifying you as a potential drug trafficker or terrorist is harmful. All the more so when the information comes in the context of a credit report, the entire purpose of which is to demonstrate that a person can be trusted.

And if this sort of confusing and frustrating communication is insufficient to establish a real injury, one wonders what could rise to that level. If, instead of falsely identifying Ramirez as a potential drug trafficker or terrorist, TransUnion had flagged him as a "potential" child molester, would that alone still be insufficient to open the courthouse doors? What about falsely labeling a person a racist? Including a slur on the report? Or what about openly reducing a person's credit score by several points because of his race? If none of these constitutes an injury in fact, how can that possibly square with our past cases indicating that the inability to "observe an animal species, even for purely esthetic purposes, . . . undeniably" is? *Lujan*, 504 U. S., at 562 . . . .

And if some of these examples do cause sufficiently "concrete" and "real"—though "intangible"—harms, how do *we* go about picking and choosing which ones do and which do not? I see no way to engage in this "inescapably value-laden" inquiry without it "devolv[ing] into [pure] policy judgment." . . . Weighing the harms caused by specific facts and choosing remedies seems to me like a much better fit for legislatures and juries than for this Court.

. . .

I respectfully dissent.

■ JUSTICE KAGAN, with whom JUSTICE BREYER and JUSTICE SOTOMAYOR join, dissenting.

. . .

. . . The Court here transforms standing law from a doctrine of judicial modesty into a tool of judicial aggrandizement. It holds, for the first time, that a specific class of plaintiffs whom Congress allowed to bring a lawsuit cannot do so under Article III. I join Justice Thomas's dissent, which explains why the majority's decision is so mistaken. As he recounts, our Article III precedents teach that Congress has broad "power to create and define rights." . . . And Congress may protect those rights by authorizing suits not only for past harms but also for the material risk of future ones. See *Spokeo*, 578 U. S., at 341–343 . . . . Under those precedents, this case should be easy. In the Fair Credit Reporting Act, Congress determined to protect consumers' reputations from inaccurate credit reporting. TransUnion willfully violated that statute's provisions by preparing credit files that falsely called the plaintiffs potential terrorists, and by obscuring that fact when the plaintiffs requested copies of their files. To say, as the majority does, that the resulting injuries did not " 'exist' in the real world" is to inhabit a world I don't know. And to make that claim in the face of Congress's contrary judgment is to exceed the judiciary's "proper—and properly limited—role." *Warth*, 422 U. S., at 498 . . . .

. . .

I differ with Justice Thomas on just one matter, unlikely to make much difference in practice. In his view, any "violation of an individual right" created by Congress gives rise to Article III standing. But in *Spokeo*, this Court held that "Article III requires a concrete injury even in the context of a statutory violation." 578 U. S., at 341. I continue to adhere to that view, but think it should lead to the same result as Justice Thomas's approach in all but highly unusual cases. As *Spokeo* recognized, "Congress is well positioned to identify [both tangible and] intangible harms" meeting Article III standards. *Ibid.* Article III requires for concreteness only a "real harm" (that is, a harm that "actually exist[s]") or a "risk of real harm." *Ibid.* And as today's decision definitively proves, Congress is better suited than courts to determine when something causes a harm or risk of harm in the real world. For that reason, courts should give deference to those congressional judgments. Overriding an authorization to sue is appropriate when but only when Congress could not reasonably have thought that a suit will contribute to compensating or preventing the harm at issue. Subject to that qualification, I join Justice Thomas's dissent in full.

PART 2

ALLOCATION OF GOVERNMENTAL POWERS: THE NATION AND THE STATES; THE PRESIDENT, THE CONGRESS, AND THE COURTS

CHAPTER 7

SEPARATION OF POWERS

3. PRESIDENTIAL CONTROL OVER THE EXECUTIVE BRANCH

Page 413. Add after Seila Law, LLC v. Consumer Financial Protection Bureau:

Collins v. Yellin

593 U.S. ___, 141 S.Ct. 1761, ___ L.Ed.2d ___ (2021).

■ JUSTICE ALITO delivered the opinion of the Court. . . .

Fannie Mae and Freddie Mac are two of the Nation's leading sources of mortgage financing. When the housing crisis hit in 2008, the companies suffered significant losses, and many feared that their troubling financial condition would imperil the national economy. To address that concern, Congress enacted the Housing and Economic Recovery Act of 2008 (Recovery Act), 122 Stat. 2654, 12 U. S. C. § 4501 *et seq.* Among other things, that law created the Federal Housing Finance Agency (FHFA), "an independent agency" tasked with regulating the companies and, if necessary, stepping in as their conservator or receiver. At its head, Congress installed a single Director, whom the President could remove only "for cause." . . .

Shortly after the FHFA came into existence, it placed Fannie Mae and Freddie Mac into conservatorship and negotiated agreements for the companies with the Department of Treasury. Under those agreements, Treasury committed to providing each company with up to $100 billion in capital, and in exchange received, among other things, senior preferred shares and quarterly fixed-rate dividends. Four years later, the FHFA and Treasury amended the agreements and replaced the fixed-rate dividend formula with a variable one that required the companies to make quarterly payments consisting of their entire net worth minus a small specified capital reserve. This deal, which the parties refer to as the "third amendment" . . . caused the companies to transfer enormous amounts of wealth to Treasury. It also resulted in a slew of lawsuits, including the one before us today.

A group of Fannie Mae's and Freddie Mac's shareholders challenged the third amendment on statutory and constitutional grounds. With respect to their statutory claim, the shareholders contended that the Agency exceeded its authority as a conservator under the Recovery Act when it agreed to a variable dividend formula that would transfer nearly all of the companies' net worth to the Federal Government. And with respect to their constitutional claim, the shareholders argued that the FHFA's structure violates the separation of powers because the Agency is led by a single Director who may be removed by the President only "for cause." . . . They sought declaratory and injunctive relief, including an order requiring Treasury either to return the variable dividend payments or to re-characterize those payments as a pay down on Treasury's investment.

We hold that the shareholders' statutory claim is barred by the Recovery Act, which prohibits courts from taking "any action to restrain or affect the exercise of [the] powers or functions of the Agency as a conservator." § 4617(f). But we conclude that the FHFA's structure violates the separation of powers, and we remand for further proceedings to determine what remedy, if any, the shareholders are entitled to receive on their constitutional claim.

I

A

. . .

The FHFA is led by a single Director who is appointed by the President with the advice and consent of the Senate. §§ 4512(a), (b)(1). The Director serves a 5-year term but may be removed by the President "for cause." § 4512(b)(2). The Director is permitted to choose three deputies to assist in running the Agency's various divisions, and the Director sits as Chairman of the Federal Housing Finance Oversight Board, which advises the Agency about matters of strategy and policy. . . . Since its inception, the FHFA has had three Senate-confirmed Directors, and in times of their absence, various Acting Directors have been selected to lead the Agency on an interim basis. . . .

. . .

II

[The Court rejected the shareholders' statutory claim. The FHFA did not exceed its authority as a conservator under the Act, and so the claim was barred by the Recovery Act's anti-injunction clause.]

. . .

III

We now consider the shareholders' claim that the statutory restriction on the President's power to remove the FHFA Director . . . is unconstitutional.

A

Before turning to the merits of this question, however, we must address threshold issues raised in the lower court or by the federal parties and appointed *amicus*.

. . .

[The Court held that the shareholders had standing to sue; a post-oral argument fourth amendment did not moot the claim for retrospective relief; a statutory "succession clause" effecting a limited transfer of stockholders' rights did not bar the suit; and the fact that the third amendment was adopted when FHFA was led by a removable-at-will Acting Director did not avoid a potential constitutional defect because the amendment's harm continued under a succession of removal-protected confirmed Directors.]

[W]e now proceed to the merits of the shareholders' constitutional argument.

B

The Recovery Act's for-cause restriction on the President's removal authority violates the separation of powers. Indeed, our decision last Term in *Seila Law* [v. CFPB] is all but dispositive. There, we held that Congress could not limit the President's power to remove the Director of the Consumer Financial Protection Bureau (CFPB) to instances of "inefficiency, neglect, or malfeasance." . . . We did "not revisit our prior decisions allowing certain limitations on the President's removal power," but we found "compelling reasons not to extend those precedents to the novel context of an independent agency led by a single Director." . . . "Such an agency," we observed, "lacks a foundation in historical practice and clashes with constitutional structure by concentrating power in a unilateral actor insulated from Presidential control." . . .

A straightforward application of our reasoning in *Seila Law* dictates the result here. The FHFA (like the CFPB) is an agency led by a single Director, and the Recovery Act (like the Dodd-Frank Act) restricts the President's removal power. Fulfilling his obligation to defend the constitutionality of the Recovery Act's removal restriction, *amicus*[a] attempts to distinguish the FHFA from the CFPB. We do not find any of these distinctions sufficient to justify a different result.

1

Amicus first argues that Congress should have greater leeway to restrict the President's power to remove the FHFA Director because the FHFA's authority is more limited than that of the CFPB. *Amicus* points out that the CFPB administers 19 statutes while the FHFA administers only 1; the CFPB regulates millions of individuals and businesses whereas the FHFA regulates a small number of Government-sponsored enterprises; the CFPB has broad rule-making and enforcement authority and the FHFA has little; and the CFPB receives a large budget from the Federal Reserve while the FHFA collects roughly half the amount from regulated entities.

We have noted differences between these two agencies. See *Seila Law*, 591 U. S., at ___ (noting that the FHFA "regulates primarily Government-sponsored enterprises, not purely private actors"). But the nature and breadth of an agency's authority is not dispositive in determining whether Congress may limit the President's power to remove its head. The President's removal power serves vital purposes even when the officer subject to removal is not the head of one of the largest and most powerful agencies. The removal power helps the President maintain a degree of control over the subordinates he needs to carry out his duties as the head of the Executive Branch, and it works to ensure that these subordinates serve the people effectively and in accordance with the policies that the people presumably elected the President to promote. . . . In addition, because the President, unlike agency officials, is elected, this control is essential to subject Executive Branch actions to a degree of electoral accountability. . . . At-will removal ensures that "the lowest officers, the middle grade, and the highest, will depend, as they ought, on the President, and the President on the community." . . . These purposes are implicated whenever an agency does important work, and nothing about the size or role of the FHFA convinces us that its Director should be treated differently from the Director of the CFPB. The test that *amicus* proposes would also lead to severe practical problems. *Amicus* does not propose any clear standard to distinguish agencies whose leaders must be removable at will from those whose leaders may be protected from at-will removal. This case is illustrative. As *amicus* points out, the CFPB might be thought to wield more power than the FHFA in some respects. But the FHFA might in other respects be considered more powerful than the CFPB.

. . .

Courts are not well-suited to weigh the relative importance of the regulatory and enforcement authority of disparate agencies, and we do not think that the constitutionality of removal restrictions hinges on such an inquiry.

. . .

[The Court rejected two other purported distinctions: "when [FHFA] steps into the shoes of a regulated entity as its conservator or receiver, it takes on the status of a private party and thus does not wield executive power," and FHFA regulates Government-sponsored enterprises rather than private actors.]

---

[a] Because the federal parties did not defend the statute's constitutionality, the Court appointed an *amicus* to do so.

4

Finally, *amicus* contends that there is no constitutional problem in this case because the Recovery Act offers only "modest [tenure] protection." That is so, *amicus* claims, because the for-cause standard would be satisfied whenever a Director "disobey[ed] a lawful [Presidential] order," including one about the Agency's policy discretion.

We acknowledge that the Recovery Act's "for cause" restriction appears to give the President more removal authority than other removal provisions reviewed by this Court. See, *e.g., Seila Law*, 591 U. S., at ___ ("for 'inefficiency, neglect of duty, or malfeasance in office' "); *Morrison* [v. Olson], 487 U. S., at 663 (" 'for good cause, physical disability, mental incapacity, or any other condition that substantially impairs the performance of [his or her] duties' "); *Bowsher* [v. Synar], *supra*, at 728 ("by joint resolution of Congress" due to " 'permanent disability,' " " 'inefficiency,' " " 'neglect of duty,' " " 'malfeasance,' " " 'a felony[,] or conduct involving moral turpitude' "); *Humphrey's Executor* v. *United States*, 295 U. S. 602, 619 (1935) (" ' "for inefficiency, neglect of duty, or malfeasance in office" ' "); *Myers* [v. United States], 272 U. S., at 107 (" 'by and with the advice and consent of the Senate' "). And it is certainly true that disobeying an order is generally regarded as "cause" for removal. See NLRB v. Electrical Workers, 346 U. S. 464, 475 (1953) ("The legal principle that insubordination, disobedience or disloyalty is adequate cause for discharge is plain enough").

But as we explained last Term, the Constitution prohibits even "modest restrictions" on the President's power to remove the head of an agency with a single top officer. *Seila Law*. . . . The President must be able to remove not just officers who disobey his commands but also those he finds "negligent and inefficient," *Myers*, 272 U.S., at 135, those who exercise their discretion in a way that is not "intelligen[t] or wis[e]," *ibid.*, those who have "different views of policy," *id.*, at 131, those who come "from a competing political party who is dead set against [the President's] agenda," *Seila Law*, . . . and those in whom he has simply lost confidence, *Myers*, *supra*, at 124. *Amicus* recognizes that " 'for cause' . . . does not mean the same thing as 'at will,' " . . . and therefore the removal restriction in the Recovery Act violates the separation of powers.

C

Having found that the removal restriction violates the Constitution, we turn to the shareholders' request for [prospective] relief. . . .

. . .

[The Court rejected the shareholders' argument that the third amendment must be completely undone because it was adopted and implemented by officers who lacked constitutional authority.] "All the officers who headed the FHFA during the time in question were properly *appointed*. Although the statute unconstitutionally limited the President's authority to *remove* the confirmed Directors, there was no constitutional defect in the statutorily prescribed method of appointment to that office. As a result, there is no reason to regard any of the actions taken by the FHFA in relation to the third amendment as void."

. . .

[With respect to the shareholders' claim that absent the unconstitutional removal restriction the President might have replaced a Director who supervised the third amendment's implementation or a Director might have behaved differently, the] "parties' arguments should be resolved in the first instance by the lower courts."

* * *

The judgment of the Court of Appeals is affirmed in part, reversed in part, and vacated in part, and the case is remanded for further proceedings consistent with this opinion.

It is so ordered.

■ JUSTICE THOMAS, concurring.

I join the Court's opinion in full. I agree that the Directors were properly appointed and could lawfully exercise executive power. And I agree that, to the extent a Government action violates the Constitution, the remedy should fit the injury. But I write separately because I worry that the Court and the parties have glossed over a fundamental problem with removal-restriction cases such as these: The Government does not necessarily act unlawfully even if a removal restriction is unlawful in the abstract.

[Justice Thomas noted the parties assumed that if the Director's removal protection is unconstitutional then the shareholders were injured by unlawful agency action. "Our recent precedents have not clearly questioned this premise, and on this premise, the Court correctly resolves the remaining legal issues. But in the future, parties and courts should ensure not only that a provision is unlawful but also that unlawful *action* was taken." Here, Justice Thomas challenged each of the shareholders' four arguments as to why the removal problem meant the agency's actions were themselves illegal; he concluded that, "absent an unlawful act, the shareholders are not entitled to a remedy." That said, Justice Thomas did "not understand the parties to have sought review of these issues in this Court," and so he invited the Fifth Circuit to "consider this issue on remand."]

. . .

■ JUSTICE KAGAN, with whom JUSTICE BREYER and JUSTICE SOTOMAYOR join as to Part II, concurring in part and concurring in the judgment in part.

Faced with a global financial crisis, Congress created the Federal Housing Finance Agency (FHFA) and gave it broad powers to rescue the Nation's mortgage market. I join the Court in deciding that the FHFA wielded its authority within statutory limits. On the main constitutional question, though, I concur only in the judgment. *Stare decisis* compels the conclusion that the FHFA's for-cause removal provision violates the Constitution. But the majority's opinion rests on faulty theoretical premises and goes further than it needs to. I also write to address the remedial question. The majority's analysis, which I join, well explains why backwards-looking relief is not always necessary to redress a removal violation. . . .

I

I agree with the majority that *Seila Law* . . . governs the constitutional question here. In *Seila Law*, the Court held that an "agency led by a single [d]irector and vested with significant executive power" comports with the Constitution only if the President can fire the director at will. 591 U. S., at ___. I dissented from that decision—vehemently. See *id.*, at ___ (Kagan, J., dissenting) ("The text of the Constitution, the history of the country, the precedents of this Court, and the need for sound and adaptable governance—all stand against the majority's opinion"). But the "doctrine of *stare decisis* requires us, absent special circumstances, to treat like cases alike"—even when that means adhering to a wrong decision. . . . So the issue now is not whether *Seila Law* was correct. The question is whether that case is distinguishable from this one. And it is not. As I observed in *Seila Law*, the FHFA "plays a crucial role in overseeing the mortgage market, on which millions of Americans annually rely." . . . It thus wields "significant executive power," much as the agency in *Seila Law* did. And I agree with the majority that there is no other legally relevant distinction between the two.

For two reasons, however, I do not join the majority's discussion of the constitutional issue. First is the majority's political theory. Throughout the relevant part of its opinion, the majority offers a contestable—and, in my opinion, deeply flawed—account of how our government should work. At-will removal authority, the majority intones, "is essential to subject Executive Branch actions to a degree of electoral accountability"—and so courts should grant the President that power in cases like this one. I see the matter differently (as, I might add, did the Framers). *Seila Law*, 591 U.S., at ___ (Kagan, J., dissenting). The right way to ensure that government operates with "electoral accountability" is to lodge decisions about its structure with, well, "the branches accountable to the people." *Id.*, at ___; see *id.*, at ___ (the Constitution "instructs Congress, not this Court, to decide on agency design"). I will subscribe to decisions contrary to my view where precedent, fairly read, controls (and there is no special justification for reversal). But I will not join the majority's mistaken musings about how to create "a workable government." *Id.*, at ___ (quoting Youngstown Sheet & Tube Co. v. Sawyer, 343 U. S. 579, 635 (1952) (Jackson, J., concurring)).

My second objection is to the majority's extension of *Seila Law*'s holding. Again and again, *Seila Law* emphasized that its rule was limited to single-director agencies "wield[ing] significant executive power." 591 U. S., at ___ (plurality opinion) . . . . To take *Seila Law* at its word is to acknowledge where it left off: If an agency did not exercise "significant executive power," the constitutionality of a removal restriction would remain an open question. . . . But today's majority careens right past that boundary line. Without even mentioning *Seila Law*'s "significant executive power" framing, the majority announces that, actually, "the constitutionality of removal restrictions" does not "hinge[ ]" on "the nature and breadth of an agency's authority." Any "agency led by a single Director," no matter how much executive power it wields, now becomes subject to the requirement of at-will removal. And the majority's broadening is gratuitous— unnecessary to resolve the dispute here. As the opinion later explains, the FHFA exercises plenty of executive authority: Indeed, it might "be considered more powerful than the CFPB." So the majority could easily have stayed within, rather than reached out beyond, the rule *Seila Law* created.

In thus departing from *Seila Law*, the majority strays from its own obligation to respect precedent. To ensure that our decisions reflect the "evenhanded" and "consistent development of legal principles," not just shifts in the Court's personnel, *stare decisis* demands something of Justices previously on the losing side. . . . They (meaning here, I) must fairly apply decisions with which they disagree. But fidelity to precedent also places demands on the winners. They must apply the Court's precedents—limits and all—wherever they can, rather than widen them unnecessarily at the first opportunity. Because today's majority does not conform to that command, I concur in the judgment only.

II

I join in full the majority's discussion of the proper remedy for the constitutional violation it finds. . . .

■ JUSTICE GORSUCH, concurring in part.

I agree with the Court on the merits and am pleased to join nearly all of its opinion. I part ways only when it comes to the question of remedy addressed in Part III-C.

[Justice Gorsuch argued that the traditional remedy for the wrongful exercise of executive authority would be to "set aside the Director's ultra vires actions as 'contrary to constitutional right,'" and this is true even where "the Director was unconstitutionally insulated from removal rather than unconstitutionally appointed." He chastised the Court for "guessing what legislative scheme Congress would have adopted in some hypothetical but-for world" and "task[ing] lower courts and the parties with reconstructing how executive agents would have reacted to it."]

. . .

. . . I would take a simpler and more familiar path. Whether unconstitutionally installed or improperly unsupervised, officials cannot wield executive power except as Article II provides. . . . [W]here individuals are burdened by unconstitutional executive action, they are "entitled to relief." . . .

■ JUSTICE SOTOMAYOR, with whom JUSTICE BREYER joins, concurring in part and dissenting in part.

Prior to 2010, this Court had gone the greater part of a century since it last prevented Congress from protecting an Executive Branch officer from unfettered Presidential removal. Yet today, for the third time in just over a decade, the Court strikes down the tenure protections Congress provided an independent agency's leadership.

Last Term, the Court held in *Seila Law* . . . that for-cause removal protection for the Director of the Consumer Financial Protection Bureau (CFPB) violated the separation of powers. As an "independent agency led by a single Director and vested with significant executive power," the Court reasoned, the CFPB had "no basis in history and no place in our constitutional structure." . . . *Seila Law* expressly distinguished the Federal Housing Finance Agency (FHFA), another independent Agency headed by a single Director, on the ground that the FHFA does not possess "regulatory or enforcement authority remotely comparable to that exercised by the CFPB." . . . Moreover, the Court found it significant that, unlike the CFPB, the FHFA "regulates primarily Government-sponsored enterprises, not purely private actors." . . .

Nevertheless, the Court today holds that the FHFA and CFPB are comparable after all, and that any differences between the two are irrelevant to the constitutional separation of powers. That reasoning cannot be squared with this Court's precedents, least of all last Term's *Seila Law*. I respectfully dissent in part from the Court's opinion and from the corresponding portions of the judgment.[1]

. . .

II

Where Congress is silent on the question, the general rule is that the President may remove Executive Branch officers at will. See Myers v. United States, 272 U. S. 52, 126 (1926). Throughout our Nation's history, however, Congress has identified particular officers who, because of the nature of their office, require a degree of independence from Presidential control. Those officers may be removed from their posts only for cause. Often, Congress has granted financial regulators such independence in order to bolster public confidence that financial policy is guided by long-term thinking, not short-term political expediency. . . . Other times, Congress has provided tenure protection to officers who investigate other Government actors and thus might face conflicts of interest if directly controlled by the President. . . .

---

[1] . . . I join also Part II of Justice Kagan's concurrence concerning the proper remedial analysis for the Fifth Circuit to conduct on remand. Finally, I note that Justice Thomas' arguments that an improper removal restriction does not necessarily render agency action unlawful warrant further consideration in an appropriate case.

In a line of decisions spanning more than half a century, this Court consistently approved of independent agencies and independent counsels within the Executive Branch. See Humphrey's Executor v. United States, 295 U. S. 602 (1935); Wiener v. United States, 357 U. S. 349 (1958); Morrison v. Olson, 487 U. S. 654 (1988). In recent years, however, the Court has taken an unprecedentedly active role in policing Congress' decisions about which officers should enjoy independence. See *Seila Law*, . . .; Free Enterprise Fund v. Public Company Accounting Oversight Bd., 561 U. S. 477 (2010). These decisions have focused almost exclusively on perceived threats to the separation of powers posed by limiting the President's removal power, while largely ignoring the Court's own encroachment on Congress' constitutional authority to structure the Executive Branch as it deems necessary.

Never before, however, has the Court forbidden simple for-cause tenure protection for an Executive Branch officer who neither exercises significant executive power nor regulates the affairs of private parties. Because the FHFA Director fits that description, this Court's precedent, separation-of-powers principles, and proper respect for Congress all support leaving in place Congress' limits on the grounds upon which the President may remove the Director.

A

In *Seila Law*, the Court held that the CFPB Director, an individual with "the authority to bring the coercive power of the state to bear on millions of private citizens and businesses," . . . must be removable by the President at will. In so holding, the Court declined to overrule *Humphrey's Executor* and *Morrison*, which respectively upheld the independence of the Federal Trade Commission's (FTC) five-member board and an independent counsel tasked with investigating Government malfeasance. See 591 U. S., at ___ ("[W]e do not revisit *Humphrey's Executor* or any other precedent today"). Instead, *Seila Law* opted not to "extend those precedents" to the CFPB, "an independent agency led by a single Director and vested with significant executive power." 591 U. S., at ___.[2]

The Court today concludes that the reasoning of *Seila Law* "dictates" that the FHFA is unconstitutionally structured because it, too, is led by a single Director. But *Seila Law* did not hold that an independent agency may never be run by a single individual with tenure protection. Rather, that decision stated, repeatedly, that its holding was limited to a single-director agency with "significant executive power." . . . The question, therefore, is not whether the FHFA is headed by a single Director, but whether the FHFA wields "significant" executive power. It does not.

. . .

. . . As the Court recognized in *Seila Law*, the FHFA does "not involve regulatory or enforcement authority remotely comparable to that exercised by the CFPB." . . . . It is in "an entirely different league" from the CFPB. 591 U. S., at ___, n. 8.

B

Because the FHFA does not possess significant executive power, the question under *Seila Law* is whether this Court's decisions upholding for-cause removal provisions in *Humphrey's Executor* and *Morrison* should be "extend[ed]" to the FHFA Director. The clear answer is yes.

---

[2] As Justice Kagan explained in dissent, *Seila Law* rested on implausible recharacterizations of this Court's separation-of-powers jurisprudence. I continue to believe that *Seila Law* was wrongly decided. Whatever the merits of that decision, however, it does not support invalidating the FHFA Director's independence.

Not only does the FHFA lack significant executive power, the authority it does possess is exercised over other governmental actors. In that respect, the FHFA Director mimics the independent counsel whose tenure protections were upheld in *Morrison*. . . .

. . .

Historical considerations further confirm the constitutionality of the FHFA Director's independence. Single-director independent agencies with limited executive power, like the FHFA, boast a more storied pedigree than do single-director independent agencies with significant executive power, like the CFPB. . . . [The Comptroller of the Currency, the Office of Special Counsel, and the Social Security Administration] provide historical support for an agency with the FHFA's limited purview.

The FHFA also draws on a long tradition of independence enjoyed by financial regulators, including the Comptroller of the Treasury, the Second Bank of the United States, the Federal Reserve Board, the Securities and Exchange Commission, the Commodity Futures Trading Commission, and the Federal Deposit Insurance Corporation. . . . The public has long accepted (indeed, expected) that financial regulators will best perform their duties if separated from the political exigencies and pressures of the present moment.

. . .

To recap, the FHFA does not wield significant executive power, the executive power it does wield is exercised over Government affiliates, and its independence is supported by historical tradition. All considerations weigh in favor of recognizing Congress' power to make the FHFA Director removable only for cause.

III

The Court disagrees. After *Seila Law*, the Court reasons, all that matters is that "[t]he FHFA (like the CFPB) is an agency led by a single Director." From that, the unconstitutionality of the FHFA Director's independence follows virtually *a fortiori*. The Court reaches that conclusion by disavowing the very distinctions it relied upon just last Term in *Seila Law* in striking down the CFPB Director's independence.

. . .

The Court's position unduly encroaches on Congress' judgments about which executive officers can and should enjoy a degree of independence from Presidential removal, and it cannot be squared with *Seila Law*, which relied extensively on such agency comparisons. . . .

. . .

. . . That the Court is unwilling to stick to the methodology it articulated just last Term in *Seila Law* is a telltale sign that the Court's separation-of-powers jurisprudence has only continued to lose its way.

IV

. . . Because I would afford Congress the freedom it has long possessed to make officers like the FHFA Director independent from Presidential control, I respectfully dissent.

United States v. Arthrex, Inc.

593 U.S. ___, 141 S.Ct. 1970 (2021).

Building on Edmond v. United States, 520 U.S. 651 (1997), the Court explored the distinction between "principal officers" and "inferior officers." Per the Appointments Clause, principal officers must be nominated by the president and confirmed by the

Senate; Congress may vest the appointment of inferior officers "in the President alone, in the Courts of Law, or in the Heads of Departments." Art. II, § 2, cl. 2.

The Patent and Trademark Office (PTO), an executive agency within the Department of Commerce, grants and issues patents in the name of the United States. The PTO has a single Director who is a principal officer, presidentially appointed and Senate confirmed. As agency head, the Director provides "policy direction and management supervision" for PTO officers and employees. Decisions about patents made by primary examiners are reviewed by the Patent Trial and Appeal Board (PTAB), an executive adjudicatory body within the PTO. The PTAB sits in panels of at least three members drawn from the Director, several senior administrators, and more than 200 Administrative Patent Judges (APJs). The APJs are appointed by the Secretary of Commerce.

Inter partes review is a process through which the PTAB can also take a second look at patents previously issued by the PTO, reconsidering whether those patents satisfy the novelty and nonobviousness requirements for inventions. The Director has unreviewable discretion to institute inter partes review. The Director designates at least three members of the PTAB (typically three APJs) to conduct such proceedings, which resemble civil litigation. The PTAB must issue a final written decision on all of the challenged patent claims within 12 to 18 months of institution. Sometimes billions of dollars hang in the balance. Losing parties may seek judicial review in the Court of Appeals for the Federal Circuit, where the Director can intervene to defend or disavow the Board's decision. The Federal Circuit reviews the PTAB's application of patentability standards *de novo* and its underlying factual determinations for substantial evidence.

In 2015, Arthrex, Inc. secured a patent on a surgical device for reattaching soft tissue to bone without tying a knot. Arthrex soon claimed that two companies had infringed the patent, and the dispute went through the PTO's inter partes review process. Three APJs formed the PTAB panel and ultimately concluded that Arthrex's own patent was invalid. On appeal to the Federal Circuit, Arthrex challenged the inter partes process on the ground that the three APJs should be considered principal officers and so their appointment by the Secretary of Commerce (rather than through presidential nomination and Senate confirmation) was unconstitutional. The Federal Circuit agreed. To remedy the violation the panel invalidated the APJs' tenure protections, concluding that making them removable at will by the Secretary of Commerce converted them into inferior officers.

Chief Justice Roberts wrote the opinion of the Court with respect to the merits of the Appointments Clause challenge, joined by Justices Alito, Gorsuch, Kavanaugh, and Barrett. These five Justices concluded that the current APJ regime is unconstitutional. The Court first connected the Appointments Clause with presidential accountability: "The President is 'responsible for the actions of the Executive Branch' and 'cannot delegate [that] ultimate responsibility or the active obligation to supervise that goes with it.' . . . The Framers recognized, of course, that 'no single person could fulfill that responsibility alone, [and] expected that the President would rely on subordinate officers for assistance.' " . . .

"Today, thousands of officers wield executive power on behalf of the President in the name of the United States. That power acquires its legitimacy and accountability to the public through 'a clear and effective chain of command' down from the President, on whom all the people vote. . . .

"Assigning the nomination power to the President guarantees accountability for the appointees' actions because the 'blame of a bad nomination would fall upon the president singly and absolutely.' The Federalist No. 77, p. 517 (J. Cooke ed. 1961) (A. Hamilton). . . ."

The Court observed that APJs are clearly officers, "not 'lesser functionaries' such as employees or contractors—because they 'exercis[e] significant authority pursuant to the laws of the United States.'" The question was whether "the nature of their responsibilities is consistent with their method of appointment" as inferior officers.

"The starting point for . . . analysis is our opinion in *Edmond*. There we explained that '[w]hether one is an "inferior" officer depends on whether he has a superior' other than the President. 520 U. S., at 662. An inferior officer must be 'directed and supervised at some level by others who were appointed by Presidential nomination with the advice and consent of the Senate.' *Id.*, at 663.

"In *Edmond*, we applied this test to adjudicative officials within the Executive Branch—specifically, Coast Guard Court of Criminal Appeals judges appointed by the Secretary of Transportation. See *id.*, at 658. We held that the judges were inferior officers because they were effectively supervised by a combination of Presidentially nominated and Senate confirmed officers in the Executive Branch . . . . 'What is significant,' we concluded, 'is that the judges of the Court of Criminal Appeals have no power to render a final decision on behalf of the United States unless permitted to do so by other Executive officers.' *Id.*, at 665.

"Congress structured the PTAB differently, providing only half of the 'divided' supervision to which judges of the Court of Criminal Appeals were subject. *Id.*, at 664. Like the Judge Advocate General, the PTO Director possesses powers of 'administrative oversight.' *Ibid.* The Director fixes the rate of pay for APJs, controls the decision whether to institute inter partes review, and selects the APJs to reconsider the validity of the patent. . . . The Director also promulgates regulations governing inter partes review, issues prospective guidance on patentability issues, and designates past PTAB decisions as 'precedential' for future panels. . . . He is the boss, except when it comes to the one thing that makes the APJs officers exercising "significant authority" in the first place— their power to issue decisions on patentability. . . . In contrast to the scheme approved by *Edmond*, no principal officer at any level within the Executive Branch 'direct[s] and supervise[s]' the work of APJs in that regard. 520 U. S., at 663.

"*Edmond* goes a long way toward resolving this dispute. What was 'significant' to the outcome there—review by a superior executive officer—is absent here: APJs have the 'power to render a final decision on behalf of the United States' without any such review by their nominal superior or any other principal officer in the Executive Branch. *Id.*, at 665. The only possibility of review is a petition for rehearing, but Congress unambiguously specified that '[o]nly the Patent and Trial Appeal Board may grant rehearings.' . . . Such review simply repeats the arrangement challenged as unconstitutional in this suit.

"This 'diffusion of power carries with it a diffusion of accountability.' . . . The restrictions on review relieve the Director of responsibility for the final decisions rendered by APJs purportedly under his charge. The principal dissent's observation that 'the Director alone has the power to take final action to cancel a patent claim or confirm it,' (opinion of Thomas, J.), simply ignores the undisputed fact that the Director's 'power' in that regard is limited to carrying out the ministerial duty that he 'shall issue and publish a certificate' canceling or confirming patent claims he had previously allowed, as dictated by the APJs' final decision. . . ."

The Court rejected as insufficient other steps the Director might take to influence the PTAB's decisionmaking process, including deciding whether or not to seek inter partes review, choosing APJs to decide a particular case whom she thinks might be predisposed to her views, vacating an unfavorable panel decision before it becomes final, and intervening in the rehearing process by again stacking the panel. But the Court viewed this as extending the problem, describing it as a "roadmap for the Director to evade a statutory prohibition on review without having him take responsibility for the ultimate decision. . . . Even if the Director succeeds in procuring his preferred outcome, such machinations blur the lines of accountability demanded by the Appointments Clause."

"Given the insulation of PTAB decisions from any executive review, the President can neither oversee the PTAB himself nor 'attribute the Board's failings to those whom he *can* oversee.' . . . APJs accordingly exercise power that conflicts with the design of the Appointments Clause 'to preserve political accountability.' *Edmond*, 520 U. S., at 663.

"The principal dissent dutifully undertakes to apply the governing test from *Edmond*, (opinion of Thomas, J.), but its heart is plainly not in it. For example, the dissent rejects any distinction between 'inferior-officer power' and 'principal-officer power,' but *Edmond* calls for exactly that: an appraisal of how much power an officer exercises free from control by a superior. The dissent pigeonholes this consideration as the sole province of the Vesting Clause, but *Edmond* recognized the Appointments Clause as a 'significant structural safeguard[ ]' that 'preserve[s] political accountability' through direction and supervision of subordinates—in other words, through a chain of command. 520 U. S., at 659, 663. The dissent would have the Court focus on the location of an officer in the agency 'organizational chart,' but as we explained in *Edmond*, '[i]t is not enough that other officers may be identified who formally maintain a higher rank, or possess responsibilities of a greater magnitude,' 520 U. S., at 662–663. The dissent stresses that 'at least two levels of authority' separate the President from PTAB decisions, but the unchecked exercise of executive power by an officer buried many layers beneath the President poses more, not less, of a constitutional problem. Conspicuously absent from the dissent is any concern for the President's ability to 'discharge his own constitutional duty of seeing that the laws be faithfully executed.' Myers v. United States, 272 U. S. 52, 135 (1926)."

The Court claimed that "[h]istory reinforces the conclusion that the unreviewable executive power exercised by APJs is incompatible with their status as inferior officers," canvassing some early congressional statutes and mid-19th century Court opinions. The Court posited that "Congress has carried the model of principal officer review into the modern administrative state," citing some examples and distinguishing others, and then tracing the history of the patent system itself.

The Court concluded:

"We hold that the unreviewable authority wielded by APJs during inter partes review is incompatible with their appointment by the Secretary to an inferior office. The principal dissent repeatedly charges that we never say whether APJs are principal officers who were not appointed in the manner required by the Appointments Clause, or instead inferior officers exceeding the permissible scope of their duties under that Clause. . . . But both formulations describe the same constitutional violation: Only an officer properly appointed to a principal office may issue a final decision binding the Executive Branch in the proceeding before us."

"In reaching this conclusion, we do not attempt to 'set forth an exclusive criterion for distinguishing between principal and inferior officers for Appointments Clause purposes." *Edmond*, 520 U. S., at 661. Many decisions by inferior officers do not bind the Executive Branch to exercise executive power in a particular manner, and we do not address supervision outside the context of adjudication. Here, however, Congress has assigned APJs 'significant authority' in adjudicating the public rights of private parties, while also insulating their decisions from review and their offices from removal."

While joining the majority opinion on the merits, Justice Gorsuch added that the Appointments Clause works hand-in-glove with the vesting of executive power in the President alone. While the framers expected the President to rely on others for help, "the framers took pains to ensure those subordinates would always remain responsible to the President and thus, ultimately, to the people. Because it is the President's duty to take care that the laws be faithfully executed, Art. II, § 3, the framers sought to ensure he possessed 'the power of *appointing, overseeing, and controlling* those who execute the laws.' 1 Annals of Cong. 463 (Madison)." In Justice Gorsuch's view, this entails that an inferior officer "must be both '*subordinate* to a[n] officer in the Executive Branch' and 'under the direct control of the President' through a 'chain of command.' *Morrison*, 487 U.S., at 720–21 (Scalia, J., dissenting)."

Justice Thomas wrote the principal dissent on the Appointments Clause merits, joined by Justices Breyer, Sotomayor, and Kagan. This dissent observed that the "Court has been careful not to create a rigid test to divide principal officers . . . from inferior ones. . . . Instead, the Court's opinions have traditionally used a case-by-case analysis. And those analyses invariably result in this Court deferring to Congress' choice of which constitutional appointment process works best." Justice Thomas read *Edmond* to create a "two-part guide": an inferior officer "must be lower in rank to 'a superior,'" and the "inferior officer's work must be 'directed and supervised at some level by others who were'" presidentially nominated and Senate confirmed. Here, the patent ALJs "are lower in rank to at least two different officers"—the PTO's Director and the Secretary of Commerce. Under *Edmond*, the fact that neither of the superiors have "complete control" does not preclude the ALJ's inferior status. And "[t]he Director here possesses even greater functional power over the Board than that possessed by the Judge Advocate General" declared an inferior officer in *Edmond*; collectively, the Director's avenues of potential control ensure that the ALJs "'have no power to render a final decision on behalf of the United States unless permitted to do so by other Executive officers.' [*Edmond*, 520 U.S.,] at 665."

Justice Thomas claimed that, under the Court's reading, "most of *Edmond* is superfluous: All that matters is whether the Director has the statutory authority to individually reverse Board decisions." But there is no precedent or historical support for this singular focus, and the "Court in *Edmond* considered all the means of supervision and control exercised by the superior officers."

"Perhaps the better way to understand the Court's opinion today is as creating a new form of intrabranch separation-of-powers law. Traditionally, the Court's task when resolving Appointments Clause challenges has been to discern whether the challenged official qualifies as a specific sort of officer and whether his appointment complies with the Constitution. . . . If the official's appointment is inconsistent with the constitutional appointment process for the position he holds, then the Court provides a remedy. . . .

"Today's majority leaves that tried-and-true approach behind. It never expressly tells us whether administrative patent judges are inferior officers or principal. And the Court never tells us whether the appointment process complies with the Constitution. The closest the Court comes is to say that 'the source of the constitutional violation' is *not* 'the appointment of [administrative patent judges] by the Secretary.' Under our precedent and the Constitution's text, that should resolve the suit. If the appointment process for administrative patent judges—appointment by the Secretary—does not violate the Constitution, then administrative patent judges must be inferior officers. See Art. II, § 2, cl. 2. And if administrative patent judges are inferior officers and have been properly appointed as such, then the Appointments Clause challenge fails. . . .

"The majority's new Appointments Clause doctrine, though, has nothing to do with the validity of an officer's appointment. Instead, it polices the dispersion of executive power among officers. Echoing our doctrine that Congress may not mix duties and powers from different branches into one actor, the Court finds that the constitutional problem here is that Congress has given a specific power—the authority to finally adjudicate inter partes review disputes—to one type of executive officer that the Constitution gives to another. . . . That analysis is doubly flawed.

"For one thing, our separation-of-powers analysis does not fit. The Constitution recognizes executive, legislative, and judicial power, and it vests those powers in specific branches. Nowhere does the Constitution acknowledge any such thing as 'inferior-officer power' or 'principal-officer power.' And it certainly does not distinguish between these sorts of powers in the Appointments Clause.

. . .

"More broadly, interpreting the Appointments Clause to bar any nonprincipal officer from taking 'final' action poses serious line-drawing problems. The majority assures that not every decision by an inferior officer must be reviewable by a superior officer. But this sparks more questions than it answers. Can a line prosecutor offer a plea deal without sign off from a principal officer? If faced with a life-threatening scenario, can an FBI agent use deadly force to subdue a suspect? Or if an inferior officer temporarily fills a vacant office tasked with making final decisions, do those decisions violate the Appointments Clause? And are courts around the country supposed to sort through lists of each officer's (or employee's) duties, categorize each one as principal or inferior, and then excise any that look problematic?

"Beyond those questions, the majority's nebulous approach also leaves open the question of how much 'principal-officer power' someone must wield before he becomes a principal officer. What happens if an officer typically engages in normal inferior-officer work but also has several principal-officer duties? . . ."

Writing further only for himself, Justice Thomas said "at some point it may be worth taking a closer look at whether the functional element of our test in *Edmond*—the part that the Court relies on today—aligns with the text, history, and structure of the Constitution. The founding era history surrounding the Inferior Officer Clause points to at least three different definitions of an inferior officer, none of which requires a case-by-case functional examination of exactly how much supervision and control another officer has. The rationales on which *Edmond* relies to graft a functional element into the inferior-officer inquiry do not withstand close scrutiny." Justice Thomas noted that "[e]arly discussions of inferior officers reflect at least three understandings of who these officers were—and who they were not—under the Appointments Clause. Though I do not purport to decide today which is best, it is worth noting that administrative patent judges would be inferior under each." Some framing discussions "divide[d] all executive officers into three categories: heads of departments, superior officers, and inferior officers." . . . Some "held a second understanding: Inferior officers encompass nearly *all* officers," other than the "Ambassadors, other public Ministers and Consuls" specifically identified in the Constitution. And some "Framers endorsed a third understanding, which distinguished just between inferior and principal officers. . . . This principal-inferior dichotomy also finds roots in the structure of the Constitution, which specifically identifies both principal officers (in the Opinions Clause and the Twenty-fifth Amendment) and inferior officers (in the Appointments Clause)." Under this view, mirrored by contemporary dictionary definitions, a " 'principal' officer is '[a] head' officer; 'a chief; not a second.' 2 Johnson, Dictionary of the English Language. Other executive officers would, by definition, be lower than or subordinate to these head officers." Justice Thomas concluded that, "[r]egardless of which of the three interpretations is correct, all lead to the same result here. Administrative patent judges are inferior officers."

Justice Breyer, joined by Justices Sotomayor and Kagan, filed another dissent on the Appointments Clause merits as well. "*First*, in my view, the Court should interpret the Appointments Clause as granting Congress a degree of leeway to establish and empower federal offices. Neither that Clause nor anything else in the Constitution describes the degree of control that a superior officer must exercise over the decisions of an inferior officer. . . ."

"*Second*, I believe the Court, when deciding cases such as these, should conduct a functional examination of the offices and duties in question rather than a formalist, judicial-rules-based approach. In advocating for a 'functional approach,' I mean an approach that would take account of, and place weight on, why Congress enacted a particular statutory limitation. It would also consider the practical consequences that are likely to follow from Congress' chosen scheme. . . . In this suit, a functional approach, which considers purposes and consequences, undermines the Court's result. . . .

   . . .

"More broadly, I see the Court's decision as one part of a larger shift in our separation-of-powers jurisprudence. The Court applied a similarly formal approach in *Free Enterprise Fund* . . . [and] *Seila Law* . . . . My dissent in the first case and Justice Kagan's dissent in the second explain in greater detail why we believed that this shift toward formalism was a mistake.

"I continue to believe that a more functional approach to constitutional interpretation in this area is superior. As for this particular suit, the consequences of the majority's rule are clear. The nature of the PTAB calls for technically correct adjudicatory decisions. . . . [T]hat fact calls for greater, not less, independence from those potentially influenced by political factors. The Court's decision prevents Congress from establishing a patent scheme consistent with that idea.

"But there are further reasons for a functional approach that extend beyond the bounds of patent adjudication. First, the Executive Branch has many different constituent bodies, many different bureaus, many different agencies, many different tasks, many different kinds of employees. Administration comes in many different shapes and sizes. Appreciating this variety is especially important in the context of administrative adjudication, which typically demands decisionmaking (at least where policy made by others is simply applied) that is free of political influence. . . .

"Second, the Constitution is not a detailed tax code, and for good reason. The Nation's desires and needs change, sometimes over long periods of time. In the 19th century the Judiciary may not have foreseen the changes that produced the New Deal, along with its accompanying changes in the nature of the tasks that Government was expected to perform. We may not now easily foresee just what kinds of tasks present or future technological changes will call for. The Founders wrote a Constitution that they believed was flexible enough to respond to new needs as those needs developed and changed over the course of decades or centuries. At the same time, they designed a Constitution that would protect certain basic principles. A principle that prevents

Congress from affording inferior level adjudicators some decisionmaking independence was not among them.

"Finally, the Executive Branch and Congress are more likely than are judges to understand how to implement the tasks that Congress has written into legislation. That understanding encompasses the nature of different mechanisms of bureaucratic control that may apply to the many thousands of administrators who will carry out those tasks. And it includes an awareness of the reasonable limits that can be placed on supervisors to ensure that those working under them enjoy a degree of freedom sufficient to carry out their responsibilities. Considered as a group, unelected judges have little, if any, experience related to this kind of a problem."

* * *

The five-Justice majority that found the PTAB's current structure to violate the Appointments Clause fractured over the appropriate remedy. No Justice agreed with the Federal Circuit's remedial order below, which would have invalidated the for-cause removal restrictions on APGs to make them removable at will by the Secretary of Commerce. Chief Justice Roberts, joined by Justices Alito, Kavanaugh, and Barrett (the "remedial plurality"), argued instead that "[i]n every respect save the insulation of their decisions from review within the Executive Branch, APJs appear to be inferior officers." So they "conclude[d] that a tailored approach is the appropriate one: Section 6(c) cannot constitutionally be enforced to the extent that its requirements prevent the Director from reviewing final decisions rendered by APJs. . . . The Director accordingly may review final PTAB decisions and, upon review, may issue decisions himself on behalf of the Board."

By contrast, Justice Gorsuch argued that, following "traditional remedial principles," the Court ought "not presume a power to 'sever' and excise portions of statutes in response to constitutional violations" but instead should "simply decline[ ] to enforce the statute in the case or controversy at hand." So here he would remedy the Appointment Clause violation merely by " 'setting aside' the PTAB decision in this case."

This fracturing created an unusual impasse, as the Court's overall lineup lacked a majority-backed disposition—four Justices would remedy the constitutional violation in one way, one Justice would remedy the violation in a different way, and four Justices found no constitutional violation and therefore would impose no remedy at all.[a] With this alignment, the Court could not issue a judgment per majority rule.

Justice Breyer (still joined by Justices Sotomayor and Kagan) broke the impasse by supporting the remedial plurality's bottom line: "For the reasons I have set forth above, I do not agree with the Court's basic constitutional determination. For purposes of determining a remedy, however, I recognize that a majority of the Court has reached a contrary conclusion. On this score, I believe that any remedy should be tailored to the constitutional violation. Under the Court's new [merits] test, the current statutory scheme is defective only because the APJ's decisions are not reviewable by the Director alone. The Court's remedy [by which Justice Breyer actually meant the solution advocated by the remedial plurality] addresses that specific problem, and for that reason I agree with its remedial holding." This created a seven-Justice coalition empowering the Director to review and supplant final PTAB decisions, even though only four of the seven sincerely believed such a remedy was necessary.

---

[a]   Justice Thomas did opine that the remedial plurality's proposed solution did not fit its characterization of the constitutional problem.

For historical examples and discussion of the propriety of such intra-case deference for strategic institutional reasons, see Caminker, *Sincere and Strategic Voting Norms on Multimember Courts*, 97 Mich.L.Rev. 2297 (1999).

PART 3

GOVERNMENT AND THE INDIVIDUAL: THE PROTECTION OF LIBERTY AND PROPERTY UNDER THE DUE PROCESS AND EQUAL PROTECTION CLAUSES

CHAPTER 9

THE DUE PROCESS, CONTRACT, AND TAKINGS CLAUSES AND THE REVIEW OF THE REASONABLENESS OF LEGISLATION

1. ECONOMIC REGULATORY LEGISLATION

C. THE TAKINGS CLAUSE OF THE FIFTH AMENDMENT—WHAT DOES IT ADD TO DUE PROCESS?

2. MANDATED ACCESS TO PROPERTY

Page 558. Delete the sentence before Dolan v. City of Tigard and add the following:

What do the following cases add?

Page 570. Add at end of subsection:

Cedar Point Nursery v. Hassid
594 U.S. ___, 141 S.Ct. 2063, ___ L.Ed.2d ___ (2021).

■ CHIEF JUSTICE ROBERTS delivered the opinion of the Court.

A California regulation grants labor organizations a "right to take access" to an agricultural employer's property in order to solicit support for unionization. Cal. Code Regs., tit. 8, § 20900(e)(1)(C) (2020). Agricultural employers must allow union organizers onto their property for up to three hours per day, 120 days per year. The question presented is whether the access regulation constitutes a *per se* physical taking under the Fifth and Fourteenth Amendments.

[The regulation promulgated by the state Agricultural Labor Relations Board required a labor organization to file a written notice with the Board and serve a copy on the employer in order to take access. It set limits on how many organizers could "enter the employer's property for up to one hour before work, one hour during the lunch break, and one hour after work"; prohibited "disruptive conduct" but otherwise allowed organizers to "meet and talk with employees as they wish"; and provided that "[i]nterference with organizers' right of access may constitute an unfair labor practice" which could "result in sanctions against the employer[.]"

[Two growers (one also a shipper), who employ hundreds of workers—none of whom live on the growers' property—sought declaratory and injunctive relief against several Board members, "argu[ing] that the access regulation effected an unconstitutional *per se* physical taking under the Fifth and Fourteenth Amendments by appropriating without compensation an easement for union organizers to enter their property." The district court ruled against the growers, and a divided Ninth Circuit affirmed.]

II

A

. . . The Founders recognized that the protection of private property is indispensable to the promotion of individual freedom. . . . This Court agrees, having noted that protection of property rights is "necessary to preserve freedom" and "empowers persons to shape and to plan their own destiny in a world where governments are always eager to do so for them." Murr v. Wisconsin . . . .

When the government physically acquires private property for a public use, the Takings Clause imposes a clear and categorical obligation to provide the owner with just compensation. . . . The government commits a physical taking when it uses its power of eminent domain to formally condemn property[,] . . . when [it] physically takes possession of property without acquiring title to it[, and] . . . when it occupies property— say, by recurring flooding as a result of building a dam. . . .

When the government, rather than appropriating private property for itself or a third party, instead imposes regulations that restrict an owner's ability to use his own property, a different standard applies. . . . To determine whether a use restriction effects a taking, this Court has generally applied the flexible test developed in *Penn Central*, ...

Our cases have often described use restrictions that go "too far" as "regulatory takings." . . . But that label can mislead. Government action that physically appropriates property is no less a physical taking because it arises from a regulation. . . . The essential question is . . . whether the government has physically taken property for itself or someone else—by whatever means—or has instead restricted a property owner's ability to use his own property. . . . Whenever a regulation results in a physical appropriation of property, a *per se* taking has occurred, and *Penn Central* has no place.

B

The access regulation appropriates a right to invade the growers' property and therefore constitutes a *per se* physical taking. The regulation grants union organizers a right to physically enter and occupy the growers' land for three hours per day, 120 days per year. Rather than restraining the growers' use of their own property, the regulation appropriates for the enjoyment of third parties the owners' right to exclude.

The right to exclude is "one of the most treasured" rights of property ownership. Loretto v. Teleprompter Manhattan CATV Corp., 458 U. S. 419, 435 (1982). . . . [W]e have stated that the right to exclude is "universally held to be a fundamental element of the property right," and is "one of the most essential sticks in the bundle of rights that are commonly characterized as property." Kaiser Aetna v. United States, 444 U. S. 164, 176, 179–180 (1979); see Dolan v. City of Tigard, 512 U. S. 374, 384, 393 (1994); Nollan v. California Coastal Comm'n, 483 U. S. 825, 831 (1987) . . . .

Given the central importance to property ownership of the right to exclude, it comes as little surprise that the Court has long treated government-authorized physical invasions as takings requiring just compensation. The Court has often described the property interest taken as a servitude or an easement.

. . .

In Loretto v. Teleprompter Manhattan CATV Corp., we made clear that a permanent physical occupation constitutes a *per se* taking regardless whether it results in only a trivial economic loss. . . .

We reiterated that the appropriation of an easement constitutes a physical taking in Nollan v. California Coastal Commission. . . .

More recently, in Horne v. Department of Agriculture, we observed that "people still do not expect their property, real or personal, to be actually occupied or taken away." 576 U. S., at 361. The physical appropriation by the government of the raisins in that case was a *per se* taking, even if a regulatory limit with the same economic impact would not have been. . . . "The Constitution," we explained, "is concerned with means as well as ends." 576 U. S., at 362.

The upshot of this line of precedent is that government-authorized invasions of property . . . are physical takings requiring just compensation. As in those cases, the government here has appropriated a right of access to the growers' property, allowing union organizers to traverse it at will for three hours a day, 120 days a year. The regulation appropriates a right to physically invade the growers' property—to literally "take access," as the regulation provides. . . . It is therefore a *per se* physical taking under our precedents. Accordingly, the growers' complaint states a claim for an uncompensated taking in violation of the Fifth and Fourteenth Amendments.

C

. . . [T]he Ninth Circuit took the view that the access regulation did not qualify as a *per se* taking because, although it grants a right to physically invade the growers' property, it does not allow for permanent and continuous access "24 hours a day, 365 days a year." . . . The dissent [concludes] likewise . . . . That position is insupportable as a matter of precedent and common sense. There is no reason the law should analyze an abrogation of the right to exclude in one manner if it extends for 365 days, but in an entirely different manner if it lasts for 364.

To begin with, we have held that a physical appropriation is a taking whether it is permanent or temporary. . . . The duration of an appropriation—just like the size of an appropriation, see *Loretto*, 458 U. S., at 436–437—bears only on the amount of compensation. . . .

. . .

Next, we have recognized that physical invasions constitute takings even if they are intermittent as opposed to continuous. *Causby* held that overflights of private property effected a taking, even though they occurred on only 4% of takeoffs and 7% of landings at the nearby airport. . . . The fact that a right to take access is exercised only from time to time does not make it any less a physical taking.

. . . [The Board's contention that] the access regulation . . . nevertheless fails to qualify as a *per se* taking because it "authorizes only limited and intermittent access for a narrow purpose[ ]" . . . is little more defensible . . . . The fact that the regulation grants access only to union organizers and only for a limited time does not transform it from a physical taking into a use restriction. . . .

The Board also takes issue with the growers' premise that the access regulation appropriates an easement. In the Board's estimation, the regulation does not exact a true easement in gross under California law because the access right may not be transferred, does not burden any particular parcel of property, and may not be recorded. This, the Board says, reinforces its conclusion that the regulation does not take a constitutionally protected property interest from the growers. The dissent agrees, suggesting that the access right cannot effect a *per se* taking because it does not require the growers to grant the union organizers an easement as defined by state property law.

These arguments misconstrue our physical takings doctrine. As a general matter, it is true that the property rights protected by the Takings Clause are creatures of state law. . . . But no one disputes that, without the access regulation, the growers would have had the right under California law to exclude union organizers from their property. . . . And no one disputes that the access regulation took that right from them. . . .

. . .

The Board and the dissent argue that PruneYard [Shopping Center v. Robins, 447 U. S. 74 (1980),] shows that limited rights of access to private property should be evaluated as regulatory rather than *per se* takings. We disagree. Unlike the growers' properties, the PruneYard was open to the public, welcoming some 25,000 patrons a day. . . . Limitations on how a business generally open to the public may treat individuals on the premises are readily distinguishable from regulations granting a right to invade property closed to the public. . . .

. . .

D

In its thoughtful opinion, the dissent advances a distinctive view of property rights. The dissent encourages readers to consider the issue "through the lens of ordinary English," and contends that, so viewed, the "regulation does not appropriate anything." Rather, the access regulation merely "*regulates* . . . the owners' right to exclude," so it must be assessed "under *Penn Central*'s fact-intensive test." . . . According to the dissent, . . . latitude toward temporary invasions is a practical necessity for governing in our complex modern world.

With respect, our own understanding of the role of property rights in our constitutional order is markedly different. In "ordinary English" "appropriation" means "*taking* as one's own," 1 Oxford English Dictionary 587 (2d ed. 1989) (emphasis added), and the regulation expressly grants to labor organizers the "right to *take* access," . . . . We cannot agree that the right to exclude is an empty formality, subject to modification at the government's pleasure. On the contrary, it is a "fundamental element of the property right," . . . that cannot be balanced away. Our cases establish that appropriations of a right to invade are *per se* physical takings, not use restrictions subject to *Penn Central* . . . . With regard to the complexities of modern society, we think they only reinforce the importance of safeguarding the basic property rights that help preserve individual liberty, as the Founders explained.

In the end, the dissent's permissive approach to property rights hearkens back to views expressed (in dissent) for decades. See, e.g., *Nollan*, 483 U. S., at 864 (Brennan, J., dissenting) . . .; *Loretto*, 458 U. S., at 455 (Blackmun, J., dissenting) . . .; *Causby*, 328 U. S., at 275 (Black, J., dissenting) . . . .

III

The Board, seconded by the dissent, warns that treating the access regulation as a *per se* physical taking will endanger a host of state and federal government activities involving entry onto private property. That fear is unfounded.

First, our holding does nothing to efface the distinction between trespass and takings. Isolated physical invasions, not undertaken pursuant to a granted right of access, are properly assessed as individual torts rather than appropriations of a property right. This basic distinction is firmly grounded in our precedent. . . .

. . .

Second, many government-authorized physical invasions will not amount to takings because they are consistent with longstanding background restrictions on property rights. As we explained in Lucas v. South Carolina Coastal Council, the government does not take a property interest when it merely asserts a "pre-existing limitation upon the land owner's title." . . . For example, the government owes a landowner no compensation for requiring him to abate a nuisance on his property, because he never had a right to engage in the nuisance in the first place. . . .

These background limitations also encompass traditional common law privileges to access private property. One such privilege allowed individuals to enter property in the event of public or private necessity. See Restatement (Second) of Torts § 196 (1964) (entry to avert an imminent public disaster); § 197 (entry to avert serious harm to a person, land, or chattels); . . . . The common law also recognized a privilege to enter property to effect an arrest or enforce the criminal law under certain circumstances. Restatement (Second) of Torts §§ 204–205. Because a property owner traditionally had no right to exclude an official engaged in a reasonable search, . . . government searches that are consistent with the Fourth Amendment and state law cannot be said to take any property right from landowners. . . .

Third, the government may require property owners to cede a right of access as a condition of receiving certain benefits, without causing a taking. In *Nollan*, we held that "a permit condition that serves the same legitimate police-power purpose as a refusal to issue the permit should not be found to be a taking if the refusal to issue the permit would not constitute a taking." 483 U. S., at 836. . . .

Under this framework, government health and safety inspection regimes will generally not constitute takings. . . . When the government conditions the grant of a benefit such as a permit, license, or registration on allowing access for reasonable health and safety inspections, both the nexus and rough proportionality requirements of the constitutional conditions framework should not be difficult to satisfy. . . .

None of these considerations undermine our determination that the access regulation here gives rise to a *per se* physical taking. Unlike a mere trespass, the regulation grants a formal entitlement to physically invade the growers' land. Unlike a law enforcement search, no traditional background principle of property law requires the growers to admit union organizers onto their premises. And unlike standard health and safety inspections, the access regulation is not germane to any benefit provided to agricultural employers or any risk posed to the public. . . . The access regulation amounts to simple appropriation of private property.

* * *

The access regulation grants labor organizations a right to invade the growers' property. It therefore constitutes a *per se* physical taking.

The judgment . . . is reversed . . . .[a]

■ JUSTICE BREYER, with whom JUSTICE SOTOMAYOR and JUSTICE KAGAN join, dissenting.

. . .

. . . [T]his regulation does not "appropriate" anything; it regulates the employers' right to exclude others. At the same time, our prior cases make clear that the regulation before us allows only a *temporary* invasion of a landowner's property and that this kind of temporary invasion amounts to a taking only if it goes "too far." . . . In my view, the

---

[a]　A concurring opinion by Justice Kavanaugh is omitted.

majority's conclusion threatens to make many ordinary forms of regulation unusually complex or impractical. And though the majority attempts to create exceptions to narrow its rule, the law's need for feasibility suggests that the majority's framework is wrong. . . .

I

. . .

A

Initially it may help to look at the legal problem . . . through the lens of ordinary English. The word "regulation" rather than "appropriation" fits this provision in both label and substance. It is contained in . . . the California Code of Regulations. It was adopted by a state regulatory board . . . in 1975. It is embedded in a set of related detailed regulations that describe and limit the access at issue. In addition to the hours of access . . ., it provides that union representatives can enter the property only "for the purpose of meeting and talking with employees and soliciting their support"; they have access only to "areas in which employees congregate before and after working" or "at such location or locations as the employees eat their lunch"; and they cannot engage in "conduct disruptive of the employer's property or agricultural operations, including injury to crops or machinery or interference with the process of boarding buses." §§ 20900(e), (e)(3), (e)(4)(C) (2021). From the employers' perspective, it restricts when and where they can exclude others from their property.

At the same time, the provision only awkwardly fits the terms "physical taking" and "physical appropriation." The "access" that it grants union organizers does not amount to any traditional property interest in land. . . .

The majority concludes that the regulation nonetheless amounts to a physical taking of property because, the majority says, it "appropriates" a "right to invade" or a "right to exclude" others. . . .

It is important to understand, however, that, technically speaking, the majority is wrong. The regulation does not *appropriate* anything. It does not take from the owners a right to invade (whatever that might mean). It does not give the union organizations the right to exclude anyone. It does not give the government the right to exclude anyone. What does it do? It gives union organizers the right temporarily to invade a portion of the property owners' land. It thereby limits the landowners' right to exclude certain others. The regulation *regulates* (but does not *appropriate*) the owners' right to exclude.

Why is it important to understand this technical point? Because only then can we understand the issue before us. That issue is whether a regulation that *temporarily* limits an owner's right to exclude others from property *automatically* amounts to a Fifth Amendment taking. Under our cases, it does not.

B

Our cases draw a distinction between regulations that provide permanent rights of access and regulations that provide nonpermanent rights of access. They either state or hold that the first type of regulation is a taking *per se*, but the second kind is a taking only if it goes "too far." . . .

. . .

. . . [T]he regulation here at issue provides access that is "temporary," not "permanent." Unlike the regulation in *Loretto*, it does not place a "fixed structure on land or real property." 458 U. S., at 437. The employers are not "forever denie[d]" "any power to control the use" of any particular portion of their property. *Id.*, at 436. And it does not totally reduce the value of any section of the property. *Ibid.* Unlike in *Nollan*, the public cannot walk over the land whenever it wishes; rather a subset of the public may enter a portion of the land three hours per day for four months per year (about 4% of the time). At bottom, the regulation here, unlike the regulations in *Loretto* and *Nollan*, is not "functionally equivalent to the classic taking in which government directly appropriates private property or ousts the owner from his domain." *Lingle*, 544 U. S., at 539.

At the same time, *PruneYard*'s holding that the taking was "temporary" (and hence not a *per se* taking) fits this case almost perfectly. There the regulation gave non-owners the right to enter privately owned property for the purpose of speaking generally to others, about matters of their choice, subject to reasonable time, place, and manner restrictions. . . . The regulation before us grants a far smaller group of people the right to enter landowners' property for far more limited times in order to speak about a specific subject. Employers have more power to control entry by setting work hours, lunch hours, and places of gathering. On the other hand, as the majority notes, the shopping center in *PruneYard* was open to the public generally. All these factors, however, are the stuff of which regulatory-balancing, not absolute *per se*, rules are made.

Our cases have recognized, as the majority says, that the right to exclude is a " 'fundamental element of the property right.' " For that reason, "[a] 'taking' may *more readily* be found when the interference with property can be characterized as a physical invasion by government." *Penn Central*, 438 U. S., at 124 (emphasis added) . . . . But a taking is not inevitably found just because the interference with property can be characterized as a physical invasion by the government, or, in other words, when it affects the right to exclude.

The majority refers to other cases. But those cases do not help its cause. That is because the Court in those cases . . . did not apply a *"per se* takings" approach. . . .

. . .

If there is ambiguity in these cases, it concerns whether the Court considered the occupation at issue to be *temporary* (requiring *Penn Central*'s "too far" analysis) or *permanent* (automatically requiring compensation). Nothing in them suggests the majority's view, namely, that compensation is automatically required for a *temporary* right of access. Nor does anything in them support the distinction that the majority gleans between "trespass" and "takings."

The majority also refers to *Nollan* as support for its claim that the "fact that a right to take access is exercised only from time to time does not make it any less a physical taking." True. Here, however, unlike in *Nollan*, the right taken is not a right to have access to the property at any time (which access different persons "exercis[e] . . . from time to time"). Rather here we have a right that does not allow access at any time. It allows access only from "time to time." And that makes all the difference. A right to enter my woods whenever you wish is a right to use that property permanently, even if you exercise that right only on occasion. A right to enter my woods only on certain occasions is not a right to use the woods permanently. In the first case one might reasonably use the term *per se* taking. It is as if my woods are yours. In the second case it is a taking only if the regulation allowing it goes "too far," considering the factors we have laid out in *Penn Central*. That is what our cases say.

Finally, the majority says that *Nollan* would have come out the same way had it involved, similar to the regulation here, access short of 365 days a year. Perhaps so. But, if so, that likely would be because the Court would have viewed the access as an "easement," and therefore an appropriation. . . . Or, perhaps, the Court would have viewed the regulation as going "too far." I can assume, purely for argument's sake, that that is so. But the law is clear: A regulation that provides *temporary*, not *permanent*, access to a landowner's property, and that does not amount to a taking of a traditional property interest, is not a *per se* taking. That is, it does not automatically require compensation. Rather, a court must consider whether it goes "too far."

C

The . . . permanent/temporary distinction . . . serves an important purpose. We live together in communities. . . . Modern life in these communities requires different kinds of regulation. Some, perhaps many, forms of regulation require access to private property (for government officials or others) for different reasons and for varying periods of time. Most such temporary-entry regulations do not go "too far." And it is impractical to compensate every property owner for any brief use of their land. . . .

Consider the large numbers of ordinary regulations in a host of different fields that, for a variety of purposes, permit temporary entry onto (or an "invasion of") a property owner's land. They include activities ranging from examination of food products to inspections for compliance with preschool licensing requirements. . . .

The majority tries to deal with the adverse impact of treating these, and other, temporary invasions as if they were *per se* physical takings by creating a series of exceptions from its *per se* rule. . . . I suspect that the majority has substituted a new, complex legal scheme for a comparatively simpler old one.

As to the first exception, what will count as "isolated"? How is an "isolated physical invasion" different from a "temporary" invasion, sufficient under present law to invoke *Penn Central*? And where should one draw the line between trespass and takings? . . .

As to the second exception, a court must focus on "traditional common law privileges to access private property." Just what are they? . . .

As to the third, what is the scope of the phrase "certain benefits"? Does it include the benefit of being able to sell meat labeled "inspected" in interstate commerce? But see *Horne*, 576 U. S., at 366 (concluding that "[s]elling produce in interstate commerce" is "not a special governmental benefit"). What about the benefit of having electricity? Of sewage collection? Of internet accessibility? Myriad regulatory schemes based on just these sorts of benefits depend upon intermittent, temporary government entry onto private property.

Labor peace (brought about through union organizing) is one such benefit, at least in the view of elected representatives. They wrote laws that led to rules governing the organizing of agricultural workers. Many of them may well have believed that union organizing brings with it "benefits," including community health and educational benefits, higher standards of living, and (as I just said) labor peace. . . . A landowner, of course, may deny the existence of these benefits, but a landowner might do the same were a regulatory statute to permit brief access to verify proper preservation of wetlands or the habitat enjoyed by an endangered species or, for that matter, the safety of inspected meat. So, if a regulation authorizing temporary access for purposes of organizing agricultural workers falls outside of the Court's exceptions and is a *per se* taking, then to what other forms of regulation does the Court's *per se* conclusion also apply?

II

Finally, I touch briefly on remedies, which the majority does not address. . . . [T]he employers do not seek compensation. They seek only injunctive and declaratory relief.

Indeed, they did not allege any damages. . . . On remand, California should have the choice of foreclosing injunctive relief by providing compensation. . . .

   . . .

PART 4

Constitutional Protection of Expression and Conscience

CHAPTER 14

RESTRICTIONS ON TIME, PLACE, OR MANNER OF EXPRESSION

4. SPEECH IN THE PUBLIC SCHOOLS

Page 1541. Add after Morse v. Frederick:

Mahanoy Area School District v. B. L.
594 U.S. ___, 141 S.Ct. 2038, ___ L.Ed.2d ___ (2021).

■ JUSTICE BREYER delivered the opinion of the Court.

A public high school student used, and transmitted to her Snapchat friends, vulgar language and gestures criticizing both the school and the school's cheerleading team. The student's speech took place outside of school hours and away from the school's campus. In response, the school suspended the student for a year from the cheerleading team. . . . Although we do not agree with the reasoning of the Third Circuit panel's majority, we do agree with its conclusion that the school's disciplinary action violated the First Amendment.

I

A

[B.L. unsuccessfully tried out for the school's varsity cheerleading squad at the end of her freshman year, though she was offered a spot on the junior varsity team. Still upset that weekend, especially since an entering freshman made the squad, at a convenience store (the Cocoa Hut) with a friend, she "used her smartphone to post two photos on Snapchat, a social media application that allows users to post photos and videos that disappear after a set period of time." Any of her roughly 250 friends in her "friend" group could "view the images for a 24 hour period."]

The first image B. L. posted showed B. L. and a friend with middle fingers raised; it bore the caption: "Fuck school fuck softball fuck cheer fuck everything." . . . The second image was blank but for a caption, which read: "Love how me and [another student] get told we need a year of jv before we make varsity but tha[t] doesn't matter to anyone else?" The caption also contained an upside-down smileyface emoji.

[Some of her Snapchat "friends" were on the squad, and at least one took pictures of her posts and shared them with other cheer squad members. In turn, one of them shared the posts with her mother, a cheerleading squad coach. As the images spread,] several cheerleaders and other students approached the . . . coaches "visibly upset" about [them]. . . . Questions about the posts persisted during an Algebra class taught by one of the two coaches. . . .

After discussing the matter with the school principal, the coaches decided that because the posts used profanity in connection with a school extracurricular activity, they violated team and school rules. As a result, the coaches suspended B. L. from the junior varsity cheerleading squad for the upcoming year. B. L.'s subsequent apologies did not move school officials. The school's athletic director, principal, superintendent, and school board, all affirmed B. L.'s suspension from the team. In response, B. L., together with her parents, filed this lawsuit in Federal District Court.

[The District Court found in B. L.'s favor. The Third Circuit affirmed, a majority of the panel concluding that because her "speech took place off campus, . . . *Tinker* . . . did not apply and the school consequently could not discipline B. L. for engaging in a form of pure speech."]

       . . .

II

We have made clear that students do not "shed their constitutional rights to freedom of speech or expression," even "at the school house gate." *Tinker*, . . . [but] we [also] have stressed . . . that schools at times stand *in loco parentis, i.e.*, in the place of parents. See Bethel School Dist. No. 403 v. Fraser, 478 U. S. 675, 684 (1986).

This Court has previously outlined three specific categories of student speech that schools may regulate in certain circumstances: (1) "indecent," "lewd," or "vulgar" speech uttered during a school assembly on school grounds, see *id.*, at 685; (2) speech, uttered during a class trip, that promotes "illegal drug use," see Morse v. Frederick, 551 U. S. 393, 409 (2007); and (3) speech that others may reasonably perceive as "bear[ing] the imprimatur of the school," such as that appearing in a school-sponsored newspaper, see *Kuhlmeier*, 484 U. S., at 271. Finally, in *Tinker*, we said schools have a special interest in regulating speech that "materially disrupts classwork or involves substantial disorder or invasion of the rights of others." 393 U. S., at 513. These special characteristics call for special leeway when schools regulate speech that occurs under its supervision.

Unlike the Third Circuit, we do not believe the special characteristics that give schools additional license to regulate student speech always disappear when a school regulates speech that takes place off campus. The school's regulatory interests remain significant in some off-campus circumstances. The parties' briefs, and those of *amici*, list several types of off-campus behavior that may call for school regulation. These include serious or severe bullying or harassment targeting particular individuals; threats aimed at teachers or other students; the failure to follow rules concerning lessons, the writing of papers, the use of computers, or participation in other online school activities; and breaches of school security devices, including material maintained within school computers.

Even B. L. herself and the *amici* supporting her would redefine the Third Circuit's off-campus/on-campus distinction, treating as on campus: all times when the school is responsible for the student; the school's immediate surroundings; travel en route to and from the school; all speech taking place over school laptops or on a school's website; speech taking place during remote learning; activities taken for school credit; and communications to school email accounts or phones. . . . And it may be that speech related to extracurricular activities, such as team sports, would also receive special treatment under B. L.'s proposed rule. . . .

We are uncertain as to the length or content of any such list of appropriate exceptions or carveouts to the Third Circuit majority's rule. . . . Particularly given the advent of computer-based learning, we hesitate to determine precisely which of many school-related off-campus activities belong on such a list. Neither do we now know how such a list might vary, depending upon a student's age, the nature of the school's off-campus activity, or the impact upon the school itself. Thus, we do not now set forth a broad, highly general First Amendment rule stating just what counts as "off campus" speech and whether or how ordinary First Amendment standards must give way off campus to a school's special need to prevent, e.g., substantial disruption of learning-related activities or the protection of those who make up a school community.

We can, however, mention three features of off-campus speech that often, even if not always, distinguish schools' efforts to regulate that speech from their efforts to regulate on-campus speech. Those features diminish the strength of the unique educational characteristics that might call for special First Amendment leeway.

First, a school, in relation to off-campus speech, will rarely stand *in loco parentis*. . . . Geographically speaking, off-campus speech will normally fall within the zone of parental, rather than school-related, responsibility.

Second, from the student speaker's perspective, regulations of off-campus speech, when coupled with regulations of on-campus speech, include all the speech a student utters during the full 24-hour day. That means courts must be more skeptical of a school's efforts to regulate off-campus speech, for doing so may mean the student cannot engage in that kind of speech at all. When it comes to political or religious speech that occurs outside school or a school program or activity, the school will have a heavy burden to justify intervention.

Third, the school itself has an interest in protecting a student's unpopular expression, especially when the expression takes place off campus. America's public schools are the nurseries of democracy. Our representative democracy only works if we protect the "marketplace of ideas." This free exchange facilitates an informed public opinion, which, when transmitted to lawmakers, helps produce laws that reflect the People's will. That protection must include the protection of unpopular ideas, for popular ideas have less need for protection. . . .

. . . Taken together, these three features of much off-campus speech mean that the leeway the First Amendment grants to schools in light of their special characteristics is diminished. We leave for future cases to decide where, when, and how these features mean the speaker's off-campus location will make the critical difference. This case can, however, provide one example.

III

Consider B. L.'s speech. Putting aside the vulgar language, the listener would hear criticism, of the team, the team's coaches, and the school—in a word or two, criticism of the rules of a community of which B. L. forms a part. This criticism did not involve features that would place it outside the First Amendment's ordinary protection. . . . To the contrary, B. L. uttered the kind of pure speech to which, were she an adult, the First Amendment would provide strong protection. . . .

Consider too when, where, and how B. L. spoke. Her posts appeared outside of school hours from a location outside the school. She did not identify the school in her posts or target any member of the school community with vulgar or abusive language. B. L. also transmitted her speech through a personal cellphone, to an audience consisting of her private circle of Snapchat friends. These features of her speech, while risking transmission to the school itself, nonetheless . . . diminish the school's interest in punishing B. L.'s utterance.

But what about the school's interest, here primarily an interest in prohibiting students from using vulgar language to criticize a school team or its coaches—at least when that criticism might well be transmitted to other students, team members, coaches, and faculty? We can break that general interest into three parts.

First, we consider the school's interest in teaching good manners and consequently in punishing the use of vulgar language aimed at part of the school community. . . . The strength of this anti-vulgarity interest is weakened considerably by the fact that B. L. spoke outside the school on her own time. . . .

B. L. spoke under circumstances where the school did not stand *in loco parentis*. And there is no reason to believe B. L.'s parents had delegated to school officials their own control of B. L.'s behavior at the Cocoa Hut. Moreover, the vulgarity in B. L.'s posts encompassed a message, an expression of B. L.'s irritation with, and criticism of, the school and cheerleading communities. Further, the school has presented no evidence of any general effort to prevent students from using vulgarity outside the classroom. Together, these facts convince us that the school's interest in teaching good manners is not sufficient, in this case, to overcome B. L.'s interest in free expression.

Second, the school argues that it was trying to prevent disruption, if not within the classroom, then within the bounds of a school-sponsored extracurricular activity. But we can find no evidence in the record of the sort of "substantial disruption" of a school activity or a threatened harm to the rights of others that might justify the school's action. *Tinker*, 393 U. S., at 514. Rather, the record shows that discussion of the matter took, at most, 5 to 10 minutes of an Algebra class "for just a couple of days" and that some members of the cheerleading team were "upset" about the content of B. L.'s Snapchats. . . . But when one of B. L.'s coaches was asked directly if she had "any reason to think that this particular incident would disrupt class or school activities other than the fact that kids kept asking . . . about it," she responded simply, "No." . . . As we said in *Tinker*, "for the State in the person of school officials to justify prohibition of a particular expression of opinion, it must be able to show that its action was caused by something more than a mere desire to avoid the discomfort and unpleasantness that always accompany an unpopular viewpoint." 393 U. S., at 509. The alleged disturbance here does not meet *Tinker*'s demanding standard.

Third, the school presented some evidence that expresses (at least indirectly) a concern for team morale. One of the coaches testified that the school decided to suspend B. L., not because of any specific negative impact upon a particular member of the school community, but "based on the fact that there was negativity put out there that could impact students in the school." . . . There is little else, however, that suggests any serious decline in team morale—to the point where it could create a substantial interference in, or disruption of, the school's efforts to maintain team cohesion. As we have previously said, simple "undifferentiated fear or apprehension . . . is not enough to overcome the right to freedom of expression." *Tinker*, 393 U. S., at 508.

It might be tempting to dismiss B. L.'s words as unworthy of the robust First Amendment protections discussed herein. But sometimes it is necessary to protect the superfluous in order to preserve the necessary. . . .

. . . The judgment . . . is . . . affirmed.

■ JUSTICE ALITO, with whom JUSTICE GORSUCH joins, concurring.

I join the opinion of the Court but write separately to explain my understanding of the Court's decision and the framework within which I think cases like this should be analyzed. . . .

. . .

. . . [W]hen a public school regulates what students say or write when they are not on school grounds and are not participating in a school program, the school has the obligation to answer the question . . .: Why should enrollment in a public school result in the diminution of a student's free-speech rights?

The only plausible answer . . . must be that by enrolling a child in a public school, parents consent on behalf of the child to the relinquishment of some of the child's free-speech rights.

. . .

When it comes to children, courts in this country have analyzed the issue of consent by adapting the common-law doctrine of *in loco parentis*. . . .

. . .

If *in loco parentis* is transplanted from Blackstone's England to the 21st century United States, what it amounts to is simply a doctrine of inferred parental consent to a public school's exercise of a degree of authority that is commensurate with the task that the parents ask the school to perform. Because public school students attend school for only part of the day and continue to live at home, the degree of authority conferred is obviously less than that delegated to the head of a late-18th century boarding school, but because public school students are taught outside the home, the authority conferred may be greater in at least some respects than that enjoyed by a tutor of Blackstone's time.

So how much authority to regulate speech do parents implicitly delegate when they enroll a child at a public school? The answer must be that parents are treated as having relinquished the measure of authority that the schools must be able to exercise in order to carry out their state-mandated educational mission, as well as the authority to perform any other functions to which parents expressly or implicitly agree—for example, by giving permission for a child to participate in an extracurricular activity or to go on a school trip.

III

. . . During the entire school day, a school must have the authority to protect everyone on its premises, and therefore schools must be able to prohibit threatening and harassing speech. . . . But even when students are on school premises during regular school hours, they are not stripped of their free-speech rights. *Tinker* teaches that expression that does not interfere with a class . . . cannot be suppressed unless it "involves substantial disorder or invasion of the rights of others." 393 U. S., at 513.

IV

A

A public school's regulation of off-premises student speech is a different matter. [T]he decision to enroll a student in a public school . . . cannot be treated as a complete transfer of parental authority over a student's speech. In our society, parents, not the State, have the primary authority and duty to raise, educate, and form the character of their children. . . . Parents do not implicitly relinquish all that authority when they send their children to a public school. . . .

B

The degree to which enrollment in a public school can be regarded as a delegation of authority over off-campus speech depends on the nature of the speech and the circumstances under which it occurs. . . . [W]ith respect to speech in each of [a few basic] groups, the question that courts must ask is whether parents who enroll their children in a public school can reasonably be understood to have delegated to the school the authority to regulate the speech in question.

One category of off-premises student speech falls easily within the scope of the authority that parents implicitly or explicitly provide. This category includes speech that takes place during or as part of what amounts to a temporal or spatial extension of the regular school program, e.g., online instruction at home, assigned essays or other homework, and transportation to and from school. Also included are statements made during other school activities in which students participate with their parents' consent, such as school trips, school sports and other extracurricular activities that may take place after regular school hours or off school premises, and after-school programs for students who would otherwise be without adult supervision during that time. Abusive speech that occurs while students are walking to and from school may also fall into this category on the theory that it is school attendance that puts students on that route and in the company of the fellow students who engage in the abuse. The imperatives that justify the regulation of student speech while in school—the need for orderly and effective instruction and student protection—apply more or less equally to these off-premises activities.

. . .

At the other end of the spectrum, there is a category of speech that is almost always beyond the regulatory authority of a public school. This is student speech that is not expressly and specifically directed at the school, school administrators, teachers, or fellow students and that addresses matters of public concern, including sensitive subjects like politics, religion, and social relations. Speech on such matters lies at the heart of the First Amendment's protection . . . .

. . .

This is true even if the student's off-premises speech on a matter of public concern is intemperate and crude. When a student engages in oral or written communication of this nature, the student is subject to whatever restraints the student's parents impose, but the student enjoys the same First Amendment protection against government regulation as all other members of the public. . . .

Between these two extremes (i.e., off-premises speech that is tantamount to on-campus speech and general statements made off premises on matters of public concern) lie the categories of off-premises student speech that appear to have given rise to the most litigation. . . .

One group of cases involves perceived threats to school administrators, teachers, other staff members, or students. Laws that apply to everyone prohibit defined categories of threats, . . . but schools have claimed that their duties demand broader authority.

Another common category involves speech that criticizes or derides school administrators, teachers, or other staff members. Schools may assert that parents who send their children to a public school implicitly authorize the school to demand that the child exhibit the respect that is required for orderly and effective instruction, but parents surely do not relinquish their children's ability to complain in an appropriate manner about wrongdoing, dereliction, or even plain incompetence. . . .

Perhaps the most difficult category involves criticism or hurtful remarks about other students. Bullying and severe harassment are serious (and age-old) problems, but these concepts are not easy to define with the precision required for a regulation of speech. . . .

V

The present case does not fall into any of these categories. Instead, it simply involves criticism (albeit in a crude manner) of the school and an extracurricular activity. Unflattering speech about a school or one of its programs is different from speech that criticizes or derides particular individuals, and for the reasons detailed by the Court . . ., the school's justifications for punishing B. L.'s speech were weak. . . .

The school did not claim that the messages caused any significant disruption of classes. . . .

. . .

. . . [F]inally, . . . whatever B. L.'s parents thought about what she did, it is not reasonable to infer that they gave the school the authority to regulate her choice of language when she was off school premises and not engaged in any school activity. And B. L.'s school does not claim that it possesses or makes any effort to exercise the authority to regulate the vocabulary and gestures of all its students 24 hours a day and 365 days a year.

. . . The overwhelming majority of school administrators, teachers, and coaches are men and women who are deeply dedicated to the best interests of their students, but it is predictable that there will be occasions when some will get carried away, as did the school officials in the case at hand. If today's decision teaches any lesson, it must be that the regulation of many types of off-premises student speech raises serious First Amendment concerns, and school officials should proceed cautiously before venturing into this territory.

■ JUSTICE THOMAS, dissenting.

. . .

. . . [S]chools historically could discipline students in circumstances like those presented here. Because the majority does not attempt to explain why we should not apply this historical rule and does not attempt to tether its approach to anything stable, I respectfully dissent.

. . .

. . . [According to Justice Thomas, 19th century cases followed this rule:] A school can regulate speech when it occurs off campus, so long as it has a proximate tendency to harm the school, its faculty or students, or its programs.

. . .

The majority . . . acknowledges that schools act *in loco parentis* when students speak on campus. But the majority fails to address the historical contours of that doctrine, whether the doctrine applies to off-campus speech, or why the Court has abandoned it.

. . . Unlike *Tinker*, . . . this case involves speech made in one location but capable of being received in countless others—an issue that has been aggravated exponentially by recent technological advances. The Court's decision not to create a solid foundation in *Tinker*, and now here not to consult the relevant history, predictably causes the majority to ignore relevant analysis.

First, the majority gives little apparent significance to B. L.'s decision to participate in an extracurricular activity. But the historical test suggests that authority of schools over off-campus speech may be greater when students participate in extracurricular programs. . . . [S]tudents like B. L. who are active in extracurricular programs have a greater potential, by virtue of their participation, to harm those programs. . . .

Second, the majority fails to consider whether schools often will have *more* authority, not less, to discipline students who transmit speech through social media. Because off-campus speech made through social media can be received on campus (and can spread rapidly to countless people), it often will have a greater proximate tendency to harm the school environment than will an off-campus in-person conversation.

Third, and relatedly, the majority uncritically adopts the assumption that B. L.'s speech, in fact, was off campus. But, the location of her speech is a much trickier question than the majority acknowledges. Because speech travels, schools sometimes may be able to treat speech as on campus even though it originates off campus. . . . [W]here it is foreseeable and likely that speech will travel onto campus, a school has a stronger claim to treating the speech as on-campus speech.

Here, it makes sense to treat B. L.'s speech as off-campus speech. There is little evidence that B. L.'s speech was received on campus. . . . But, the majority . . . bypasses this relevant inquiry.

* * *

The Court . . . states just one rule: Schools can regulate speech less often when that speech occurs off campus. . . . But . . . courts (and schools) will almost certainly be at a loss as to what exactly the Court's opinion today means.

. . .

CHAPTER 15

PROTECTION OF PENUMBRAL FIRST AMENDMENT RIGHTS

2. FREEDOM OF ASSOCIATION

A. INTRODUCTION

Page 1598. Add after NAACP v. Alabama:

Americans for Prosperity Foundation v. Bonta
594 U.S. ___, 141 S.Ct. 2373, ___ L.Ed.2d ___ (2021).

■ CHIEF JUSTICE ROBERTS delivered the opinion of the Court, except as to Part II-B-1.

To solicit contributions in California, charitable organizations must disclose to the state Attorney General's Office the identities of their major donors. The State contends that having this information on hand makes it easier to police misconduct by charities. We must decide whether California's disclosure requirement violates the First Amendment right to free association.

I

The California Attorney General's Office is responsible for statewide law enforcement, including the supervision and regulation of charitable fundraising. Under state law, the Attorney General is authorized to "establish and maintain a register" of charitable organizations and to obtain "whatever information, copies of instruments, reports, and records are needed for the establishment and maintenance of the register." Cal. Govt. Code Ann. § 12584 (West 2018). In order to operate and raise funds in California, charities generally must register with the Attorney General and renew their registrations annually. . . . Over 100,000 charities are currently registered in the State, and roughly 60,000 renew their registrations each year.

California law empowers the Attorney General to make rules and regulations regarding the registration and renewal process. . . . Pursuant to this regulatory authority, the Attorney General requires charities renewing their registrations to file copies of their Internal Revenue Service Form 990, along with any attachments and schedules. . . . Form 990 contains information regarding tax-exempt organizations' mission, leadership, and finances. Schedule B to Form 990—the document that gives rise to the present dispute—requires organizations to disclose the names and addresses of donors who have contributed more than $5,000 in a particular tax year (or, in some cases, who have given more than 2 percent of an organization's total contributions). . . .

The petitioners are tax-exempt charities that solicit contributions in California and are subject to the Attorney General's registration and renewal requirements. Americans for Prosperity Foundation is a public charity that is "devoted to education and training about the principles of a free and open society, including free markets, civil liberties, immigration reform, and constitutionally limited government." . . . Thomas More Law Center is a public interest law firm whose "mission is to protect religious freedom, free speech, family values, and the sanctity of human life." . . . Since 2001, each petitioner has renewed its registration and has filed a copy of its Form 990 with the Attorney General, as required by [California law]. Out of concern for their donors' anonymity, however, the petitioners have declined to file their Schedule Bs (or have filed only redacted versions) with the State.

For many years, the petitioners' reluctance to turn over donor information presented no problem because the Attorney General was not particularly zealous about collecting Schedule Bs. That changed in 2010, when the California Department of Justice "ramped up its efforts to enforce charities' Schedule B obligations, sending thousands of deficiency letters to charities that had not complied with the Schedule B requirement." . . . The Law Center and the Foundation received deficiency letters in 2012 and 2013, respectively. When they continued to resist disclosing their contributors' identities, the Attorney General threatened to suspend their registrations and fine their directors and officers.

The petitioners each responded by filing suit in the Central District of California. In their complaints, they alleged that the Attorney General had violated their First Amendment rights and the rights of their donors. The petitioners alleged that disclosure of their Schedule Bs would make their donors less likely to contribute and would subject them to the risk of reprisals. Both organizations challenged the disclosure requirement on its face and as applied to them.

In each case, the District Court granted preliminary injunctive relief prohibiting the Attorney General from collecting their Schedule B information. . . . The Ninth Circuit vacated and remanded. . . . The court held that it was bound by Circuit precedent to reject the petitioners' facial challenge. . . . And reviewing the petitioners' as-applied claims under an "exacting scrutiny" standard, the panel narrowed the injunction, allowing the Attorney General to collect the petitioners' Schedule Bs so long as he did not publicly disclose them. . . .

On remand, the District Court held bench trials in both cases, after which it entered judgment for the petitioners and permanently enjoined the Attorney General from collecting their Schedule Bs. . . . Applying exacting scrutiny, the District Court held that disclosure of Schedule Bs was not narrowly tailored to the State's interest in investigating charitable misconduct. The court credited testimony from California officials that Schedule Bs were rarely used to audit or investigate charities. And it found that even where Schedule B information was used, that information could be obtained from other sources.

The court also determined that the disclosure regime burdened the associational rights of donors. In both cases, the court found that the petitioners had suffered from threats and harassment in the past, and that donors were likely to face similar retaliation in the future if their affiliations became publicly known. For example, the CEO of the Foundation testified that a technology contractor working at the Foundation's headquarters had posted online that he was "inside the belly of the beast" and "could easily walk into [the CEO's] office and slit his throat." . . . And the Law Center introduced evidence that it had received "threats, harassing calls, intimidating and obscene emails, and even pornographic letters." . . .

The District Court also found that California was unable to ensure the confidentiality of donors' information. During the course of litigation, the Foundation identified nearly 2,000 confidential Schedule Bs that had been inadvertently posted to the Attorney General's website, including dozens that were found the day before trial. One of the Foundation's expert witnesses also discovered that he was able to access hundreds of thousands of confidential documents on the website simply by changing a digit in the URL. The court found after trial that "the amount of careless mistakes made by the Attorney General's Registry is shocking." ... And although California subsequently codified a policy prohibiting disclosure ...—an effort the District Court described as "commendable"—the court determined that "[d]onors and potential donors would be reasonably justified in a fear of disclosure given such a context" of past breaches. ...

The Ninth Circuit again vacated the District Court's injunctions, and this time reversed the judgments and remanded for entry of judgment in favor of the Attorney General. ... The court held that the District Court had erred by imposing a narrow tailoring requirement. ... And it reasoned that the disclosure regime satisfied exacting scrutiny because the up-front collection of charities' Schedule Bs promoted investigative efficiency and effectiveness. ... The panel also found that the disclosure of Schedule Bs would not meaningfully burden donors' associational rights, in part because the Attorney General had taken remedial security measures to fix the confidentiality breaches identified at trial. ...

. . .

We granted certiorari. ...

II

A

The First Amendment prohibits government from "abridging the freedom of speech, or of the press; or the right of the people peaceably to assemble, and to petition the Government for a redress of grievances." This Court has "long understood as implicit in the right to engage in activities protected by the First Amendment a corresponding right to associate with others." Roberts v. United States Jaycees, 468 U.S. 609, 622 (1984). Protected association furthers "a wide variety of political, social, economic, educational, religious, and cultural ends," and "is especially important in preserving political and cultural diversity and in shielding dissident expression from suppression by the majority." *Ibid.* Government infringement of this freedom "can take a number of forms." *Ibid.* We have held, for example, that the freedom of association may be violated where a group is required to take in members it does not want, see *id.*, at 623, where individuals are punished for their political affiliation, see Elrod v. Burns, 427 U.S. 347, 355 (1976) (plurality opinion), or where members of an organization are denied benefits based on the organization's message, see Healy v. James, 408 U.S. 169, 181–182 (1972).

We have also noted that "[i]t is hardly a novel perception that compelled disclosure of affiliation with groups engaged in advocacy may constitute as effective a restraint on freedom of association as [other] forms of governmental action." NAACP v. Alabama ex rel. Patterson, 357 U.S. 449, 462 (1958). NAACP v. Alabama involved this chilling effect in its starkest form. The NAACP opened an Alabama office that supported racial integration in higher education and public transportation. ... In response, NAACP members were threatened with economic reprisals and violence. ... As part of an effort to oust the organization from the State, the Alabama Attorney General sought the group's membership lists. ... We held that the First Amendment prohibited such compelled disclosure. ... We explained that "[e]ffective advocacy of both public and private points of view, particularly controversial ones, is undeniably enhanced by group association," *id.*, at 460, and we noted "the vital relationship between freedom to associate and privacy in one's associations," *id.*, at 462. Because NAACP members faced a risk of reprisals if their affiliation with the organization became known—and because Alabama had demonstrated no offsetting interest "sufficient to justify the deterrent effect" of disclosure . . .—we concluded that the State's demand violated the First Amendment.

B

1

NAACP v. Alabama did not phrase in precise terms the standard of review that applies to First Amendment challenges to compelled disclosure. We have since settled on a standard referred to as "exacting scrutiny." Buckley v. Valeo, 424 U.S. 1, 64 (1976) (*per curiam*). Under that standard, there must be "a substantial relation between the disclosure requirement and a sufficiently important governmental interest." Doe v. Reed, 561 U.S. 186 (2010) (internal quotation marks omitted). "To withstand this scrutiny, the strength of the governmental interest must reflect the seriousness of the actual burden on First Amendment rights." . . . (internal quotation marks omitted). Such scrutiny, we have held, is appropriate given the "deterrent effect on the exercise of First Amendment rights" that arises as an "inevitable result of the government's conduct in requiring disclosure." *Buckley*, 424 U.S., at 65.

The Law Center (but not the Foundation) argues that we should apply strict scrutiny, not exacting scrutiny. Under strict scrutiny, the government must adopt "the least restrictive means of achieving a compelling state interest," McCullen v. Coakley, 573 U.S. 464, 478 (2014), rather than a means substantially related to a sufficiently important interest. The Law Center contends that only strict scrutiny adequately protects the associational rights of charities. And although the Law Center acknowledges that we have applied exacting scrutiny in prior disclosure cases, it argues that those cases arose in the electoral context, where the government's important interests justify less searching review.

It is true that we first enunciated the exacting scrutiny standard in a campaign finance case. See *Buckley*, 424 U.S., at 64–68. And we have since invoked it in other election-related settings. See, *e.g.*, Citizens United v. Federal Election Comm'n, 558 U.S. 310, 366–367 (2010); Davis v. Federal Election Comm'n, 554 U.S. 724, 744 (2008). But exacting scrutiny is not unique to electoral disclosure regimes. To the contrary, *Buckley* derived the test from NAACP v. Alabama itself, as well as other nonelection cases. See 424 U.S., at 64 [citations omitted]. As we explained in NAACP v. Alabama, "it is immaterial" to the level of scrutiny "whether the beliefs sought to be advanced by association pertain to political, economic, religious or cultural matters." 357 U.S., at 460–461. Regardless of the type of association, compelled disclosure requirements are reviewed under exacting scrutiny.

2

The Law Center (now joined by the Foundation) argues in the alternative that even if exacting scrutiny applies, such review incorporates a least restrictive means test similar to the one imposed by strict scrutiny. The United States and the Attorney General respond that exacting scrutiny demands no additional tailoring beyond the "substantial relation" requirement noted above. We think that the answer lies between those two positions. While exacting scrutiny does not require that disclosure regimes be the least restrictive means of achieving their ends, it does require that they be narrowly tailored to the government's asserted interest.

The need for narrow tailoring was set forth early in our compelled disclosure cases. In Shelton v. Tucker, we considered an Arkansas statute that required teachers to disclose every organization to which they belonged or contributed. 364 U.S., at 480. We acknowledged the importance of "the right of a State to investigate the competence and fitness of those whom it hires to teach in its schools." *Id.*, at 485. On that basis, we distinguished prior decisions in which we had found "no substantially relevant correlation between the governmental interest asserted and the State's effort to compel disclosure." *Ibid.* But we nevertheless held that the Arkansas statute was invalid because even a "legitimate and substantial" governmental interest "cannot be pursued by means that broadly stifle fundamental personal liberties when the end can be more narrowly achieved." . . .; see also Louisiana ex rel. Gremillion v. NAACP, 366 U.S. 293, 296, (1961) (quoting same).

Shelton stands for the proposition that a substantial relation to an important interest is not enough to save a disclosure regime that is insufficiently tailored. This requirement makes sense. Narrow tailoring is crucial where First Amendment activity is chilled—even if indirectly—"[b]ecause First Amendment freedoms need breathing space to survive." . . .

Our more recent decisions confirm the need for tailoring. In McCutcheon v. Federal Election Commission, 572 U.S. 185 (2014), for example, a plurality of the Court explained:

> "In the First Amendment context, fit matters. Even when the Court is not applying strict scrutiny, we still require a fit that is not necessarily perfect, but reasonable; that represents not necessarily the single best disposition but one whose scope is in proportion to the interest served, that employs not necessarily the least restrictive means but a means narrowly tailored to achieve the desired objective." *Id.*, at 218 (internal quotation marks and alterations omitted).

McCutcheon is instructive here. A substantial relation is necessary but not sufficient to ensure that the government adequately considers the potential for First Amendment harms before requiring that organizations reveal sensitive information about their members and supporters. Where exacting scrutiny applies, the challenged requirement must be narrowly tailored to the interest it promotes, even if it is not the least restrictive means of achieving that end.

. . .

III

. . .

A

As explained, exacting scrutiny requires that there be "a substantial relation between the disclosure requirement and a sufficiently important governmental interest," . . . and that the disclosure requirement be narrowly tailored to the interest it promotes. . . . The Ninth Circuit found that there was a substantial relation between the Attorney General's demand for Schedule Bs and a sufficiently strong governmental interest. . . . Of particular relevance, the court found that California had such an interest in preventing charitable fraud and self-dealing, and that "the up-front collection of Schedule B information improves the efficiency and efficacy of the Attorney General's important regulatory efforts." . . . The court did not apply a narrow tailoring requirement, however, because it did not read our cases to mandate any such inquiry. . . . That was error. And properly applied, the narrow tailoring requirement is not satisfied by the disclosure regime.

We do not doubt that California has an important interest in preventing wrongdoing by charitable organizations. It goes without saying that there is a "substantial governmental interest[ ] in protecting the public from fraud." . . . The Attorney General receives complaints each month that identify a range of misconduct, from "misuse, misappropriation, and diversion of charitable assets," to "false and misleading charitable solicitations," to other "improper activities by charities soliciting charitable donations." . . . Such offenses cause serious social harms. And the Attorney General is the primary law enforcement officer charged with combating them under California law. . . .

There is a dramatic mismatch, however, between the interest that the Attorney General seeks to promote and the disclosure regime that he has implemented in service of that end. Recall that 60,000 charities renew their registrations each year, and nearly all are required to file a Schedule B. Each Schedule B, in turn, contains information about a charity's top donors—a small handful of individuals in some cases, but hundreds in others. . . . This information includes donors' names and the total contributions they have made to the charity, as well as their addresses.

Given the amount and sensitivity of this information harvested by the State, one would expect Schedule B collection to form an integral part of California's fraud detection efforts. It does not. To the contrary, the record amply supports the District Court's finding that there was not "a single, concrete instance in which pre-investigation collection of a Schedule B did anything to advance the Attorney General's investigative, regulatory or enforcement efforts.". . .

. . .

The Attorney General and the dissent contend that alternative means of obtaining Schedule B information—such as a subpoena or audit letter—are inefficient and ineffective compared to up-front collection. . . . It became clear at trial, however, that the Office had not even considered alternatives to the current disclosure requirement. . . . The Attorney General and the dissent also argue that a targeted request for Schedule B information could tip a charity off, causing it to "hide or tamper with evidence." . . . But again, the States' witnesses failed to substantiate that concern. . . . Furthermore, even if tipoff were a concern in some cases, the State's indiscriminate collection of Schedule Bs in all cases would not be justified.

The upshot is that California casts a dragnet for sensitive donor information from tens of thousands of charities each year, even though that information will become relevant in only a small number of cases involving filed complaints. . . . California does not rely on Schedule Bs to initiate investigations, and in all events, there are multiple alternative mechanisms through which the Attorney General can obtain Schedule B information after initiating an investigation. The need for up-front collection is particularly dubious given that California—one of only three States to impose such a requirement . . . —did not rigorously enforce the disclosure obligation until 2010. . . .

In reality, then, California's interest is less in investigating fraud and more in ease of administration. This interest, however, cannot justify the disclosure requirement. The Attorney General may well prefer to have every charity's information close at hand, just in case. But "the prime objective of the First Amendment is not efficiency." . . . Mere administrative convenience does not remotely "reflect the seriousness of the actual burden" that the demand for Schedule Bs imposes on donors' association rights. . . .

B

The foregoing discussion also makes clear why a facial challenge is appropriate in these cases. Normally, a plaintiff bringing a facial challenge must "establish that no set of circumstances exists under which the [law] would be valid,", . . . or show that the law lacks "a plainly legitimate sweep," . . . In the First Amendment context, however, we have recognized "a second type of facial challenge, whereby a law may be invalidated as overbroad if a substantial number of its applications are unconstitutional, judged in relation to the statute's plainly legitimate sweep.". . . . We have no trouble concluding here that the Attorney General's disclosure requirement is overbroad. The lack of tailoring to the State's investigative goals is categorical—present in every case—as is the weakness of the State's interest in administrative convenience. Every demand that might chill association therefore fails exacting scrutiny.

The Attorney General tries to downplay the burden on donors, arguing that "there is no basis on which to conclude that California's requirement results in any broad-based chill." He emphasizes that "California's Schedule B requirement is confidential," and he suggests that certain donors—like those who give to noncontroversial charities—are unlikely to be deterred from contributing. . . . . He also contends that disclosure to his office imposes no added burdens on donors because tax-exempt charities already provide their Schedule Bs to the IRS. . . .

We are unpersuaded. Our cases have said that disclosure requirements can chill association "[e]ven if there [is] no disclosure to the general public." . . . In *Shelton*, for example, we noted the "constant and heavy" pressure teachers would experience simply by disclosing their associational ties to their schools. . . . Exacting scrutiny is triggered by "state action which *may* have the effect of curtailing the freedom to associate," and by the "*possible* deterrent effect" of disclosure. NAACP v. Alabama, 357 U.S., at 460–461 (emphasis added); see Talley v. California, 362 U.S. 60, 65 (1960) ("identification and fear of reprisal *might* deter perfectly peaceful discussions of public matters of importance" (emphasis added)). While assurances of confidentiality may reduce the burden of disclosure to the State, they do not eliminate it.

It is irrelevant, moreover, that some donors might not mind—or might even prefer—the disclosure of their identities to the State. The disclosure requirement "creates an unnecessary risk of chilling" in violation of the First Amendment, . . ., indiscriminately sweeping up the information of *every* major donor with reason to remain anonymous. The petitioners here, for example, introduced evidence that they and their supporters have been subjected to bomb threats, protests, stalking, and physical violence. . . . Such risks are heightened in the 21st century and seem to grow with each passing year, as "anyone with access to a computer [can] compile a wealth of information about" anyone else, including such sensitive details as a person's home address or the school attended by his children. . . .

The gravity of the privacy concerns in this context is further underscored by the filings of hundreds of organizations as *amici curiae* in support of the petitioners. Far from representing uniquely sensitive causes, these organizations span the ideological spectrum, and indeed the full range of human endeavors: from the American Civil Liberties Union to the Proposition 8 Legal Defense Fund; from the Council on American-Islamic Relations to the Zionist Organization of America; from Feeding America—Eastern Wisconsin to PBS Reno. The deterrent effect feared by these organizations is real and pervasive, even if their concerns are not shared by every single charity operating or raising funds in California.

. . .

Finally, California's demand for Schedule Bs cannot be saved by the fact that donor information is already disclosed to the IRS as a condition of federal tax-exempt status. For one thing, each governmental demand for disclosure brings with it an additional risk of chill. For another, revenue collection efforts and conferral of tax-exempt status may raise issues not presented by California's disclosure requirement, which can prevent charities from operating in the State altogether. . . .

. . .

The District Court correctly entered judgment in favor of the petitioners and permanently enjoined the Attorney General from collecting their Schedule Bs. The Ninth Circuit erred by vacating those injunctions and directing entry of judgment for the Attorney General. The judgment of the Ninth Circuit is reversed, and the cases are remanded for further proceedings consistent with this opinion.

It is so ordered.

■ JUSTICE THOMAS, concurring in Parts I, II-A, II-B-2, and III-A, and concurring in the judgment.

The Court correctly holds that California's disclosure requirement violates the First Amendment. It also correctly concludes that the District Court properly enjoined California's attorney general from collecting the forms at issue, which contain sensitive donor information. But, while I agree with much of the Court's opinion, I would approach three issues differently.

First, the bulk of "our precedents . . . require application of strict scrutiny to laws that compel disclosure of protected First Amendment association." . . .

Second, the Court holds the law "overbroad" and, thus, invalid in all circumstances. . . . But I continue to have "doubts about [the] origins and application" of our "overbreadth doctrine." . . .

Third, and relatedly, this Court also lacks the power "to 'pronounce that the statute is unconstitutional in *all* applications,'" even if the Court suspects that the law will likely be unconstitutional in every future application as opposed to just a substantial number of its applications. . . . A declaration that the law is "facially" unconstitutional "seems to me no more than an advisory opinion—which a federal court should never issue at all." . . . Courts cannot "strike down statutory text" or resolve the legal rights of litigants not before them. . . .

Despite the Court's use of the term "facially unconstitutional," I join Part III-A, which finds that California's law fails exacting scrutiny, because the Court does not say that it is "provid[ing] relief beyond the parties to the case." . . .

With those points of difference clarified, I join Parts I, II-A, II-B-2, and III-A of the majority's opinion and concur in the judgment.

■ JUSTICE ALITO, with whom JUSTICE GORSUCH joins, concurring in Parts I, II-A, II-B-2, and III, and concurring in the judgment.

I am pleased to join most of THE CHIEF JUSTICE'S opinion. In particular, I agree that the exacting scrutiny standard drawn from our election-law jurisprudence has real teeth. It requires both narrow tailoring and consideration of alternative means of obtaining the sought-after information. . . . For the reasons THE CHIEF JUSTICE explains, California's blunderbuss approach to charitable disclosures fails exacting scrutiny and is facially unconstitutional. . . . The question is not even close. And for the same reasons, California's approach necessarily fails strict scrutiny.

THE CHIEF JUSTICE would hold that the particular exacting scrutiny standard in our election-law jurisprudence applies categorically "to First Amendment challenges to compelled disclosure." . . . JUSTICE THOMAS, by contrast, would hold that strict scrutiny applies in all such cases. . . . I am not prepared at this time to hold that a single standard applies to all disclosure requirements. And I do not read our cases to have broadly resolved the question in favor of exacting scrutiny. . . .

Because the choice between exacting and strict scrutiny has no effect on the decision in these cases, I see no need to decide which standard should be applied here or whether the same level of scrutiny should apply in all cases in which the compelled disclosure of associations is challenged under the First Amendment.

■ JUSTICE SOTOMAYOR, with whom JUSTICE BREYER and JUSTICE KAGAN join, dissenting.

Although this Court is protective of First Amendment rights, it typically requires that plaintiffs demonstrate an actual First Amendment burden before demanding that a law be narrowly tailored to the government's interests, never mind striking the law down in its entirety. Not so today. Today, the Court holds that reporting and disclosure requirements must be narrowly tailored even if a plaintiff demonstrates no burden at all. The same scrutiny the Court applied when NAACP members in the Jim Crow South did not want to disclose their membership for fear of reprisals and violence now applies equally in the case of donors only too happy to publicize their names across the websites and walls of the organizations they support.

California oversees nearly a quarter of this Nation's charitable assets. As part of that oversight, it investigates and prosecutes charitable fraud, relying in part on a registry where it collects and keeps charitable organizations' tax forms. The majority holds that a California regulation requiring charitable organizations to disclose tax forms containing the names and contributions of their top donors unconstitutionally burdens the right to associate even if the forms are not publicly disclosed.

In so holding, the Court discards its decades-long requirement that, to establish a cognizable burden on their associational rights, plaintiffs must plead and prove that disclosure will likely expose them to objective harms, such as threats, harassment, or reprisals. It also departs from the traditional, nuanced approach to First Amendment challenges, whereby the degree of means-end tailoring required is commensurate to the actual burdens on associational rights. Finally, it recklessly holds a state regulation facially invalid despite petitioners' failure to show that a substantial proportion of those affected would prefer anonymity, much less that they are objectively burdened by the loss of it.

Today's analysis marks reporting and disclosure requirements with a bull's-eye. Regulated entities who wish to avoid their obligations can do so by vaguely waving toward First Amendment "privacy concerns." ... It does not matter if not a single individual risks experiencing a single reprisal from disclosure, or if the vast majority of those affected would happily comply. That is all irrelevant to the Court's determination that California's Schedule B requirement is facially unconstitutional. Neither precedent nor common sense supports such a result. I respectfully dissent.

. . .

CHAPTER 17

RELIGION AND THE CONSTITUTION

2. THE FREE EXERCISE OF RELIGION

Page 1874. Replace Roman Catholic Diocese of Brooklyn v. Cuomo with the following:

Tandon v. Newsom, 593 U.S. ___, 141 S.Ct. 1294 (2021). To combat the spread of COVID-19 during the global coronavirus pandemic, California restricted at-home gatherings to no more than three households, at least for a period of time. Plaintiffs sought a preliminary injunction against application of this restriction to at-home religious exercises in larger groups. The district court denied their motion, and the Ninth Circuit denied their application for emergency injunctive relief pending appeal. The Supreme Court granted the latter request, however, in a 5–4 per curiam ruling. The majority opinion said in relevant part:

"The Ninth Circuit's failure to grant an injunction pending appeal was erroneous. This Court's decisions have made the following points clear.

"First, government regulations are not neutral and generally applicable, and therefore trigger strict scrutiny under the Free Exercise Clause, whenever they treat *any* comparable secular activity more favorably than religious exercise. Roman Catholic Diocese of Brooklyn v. Cuomo, 592 U. S. ___, ___–___ (2020) (per curiam) . . . . It is no answer that a State treats some comparable secular businesses or other activities as poorly as or even less favorably than the religious exercise at issue. . . .[a]

"Second, whether two activities are comparable for purposes of the Free Exercise Clause must be judged against the asserted government interest that justifies the regulation at issue. Id., at ___ . . . (describing secular activities treated more favorably than religious worship that either 'have contributed to the spread of COVID-19' or 'could' have presented similar risks). Comparability is concerned with the risks various activities pose, not the reasons why people gather. . . .

---

[a] The *Roman Catholic Diocese* case involved capacity restrictions in *public* spaces, including churches and businesses. With the same 5–4 division among the Justices, the per curiam majority there also had granted emergency injunctive relief pending appeal, the majority concluding that the "regulations cannot be viewed as neutral because they single out houses of worship for especially harsh treatment" compared to lesser capacity restrictions on "essential" and "even nonessential" businesses. Chief Justice Roberts would have avoided granting injunctive relief, because the Governor had "revised the designations of the affected areas" and "it is a significant matter to override determinations made by public health officials concerning what is necessary for public safety in the midst of a deadly pandemic"— even though he thought the numerical capacity limits "do seem unduly restrictive" and "may well . . . violate the Free Exercise Clause." A dissent by Justice Breyer, joined by Justices Sotomayor and Kagan, agreed that there was "no need now to issue [the] injunction[,]" but also thought the merits of the free exercise claim were "far from clear[.]" And Justice Sotomayor's separate dissent, joined by Justice Kagan, thought the regulations treated "religious institutions equally or more favorably than comparable secular institutions" like concerts, movie showings, lectures and sporting events, which were subject to more restrictive capacity limits. Businesses were dissimilar in her view, because religious services involved "large groups of people gathering, speaking, and singing in close proximity indoors for extended periods of time."

"Third, the government has the burden to establish that the challenged law satisfies strict scrutiny. To do so in this context, . . . narrow tailoring requires the government to show that measures less restrictive of the First Amendment activity could not address its interest in reducing the spread of COVID. Where the government permits other activities to proceed with precautions, it must show that the religious exercise at issue is more dangerous than those activities even when the same precautions are applied. Otherwise, precautions that suffice for other activities suffice for religious exercise too. . . .

"Fourth, even if the government withdraws or modifies a COVID restriction in the course of litigation, that does not necessarily moot the case. And so long as a case is not moot, litigants otherwise entitled to emergency injunctive relief remain entitled to such relief where the applicants 'remain under a constant threat' that government officials will use their power to reinstate the challenged restrictions. . . .

"These principles dictated the outcome in this case . . . . First, California treats some comparable secular activities more favorably than at-home religious exercise, permitting hair salons, retail stores, personal care services, movie theaters, private suites at sporting events and concerts, and indoor restaurants to bring together more than three households at a time. . . . Second, the Ninth Circuit did not conclude that those activities pose a lesser risk of transmission than applicants' proposed religious exercise at home. The Ninth Circuit erroneously rejected these comparators simply because this Court's previous decisions involved public buildings as opposed to private buildings. . . . Third, instead of requiring the State to explain why it could not safely permit at-home worshipers to gather in larger numbers while using precautions used in secular activities, the Ninth Circuit erroneously declared that such measures might not 'translate readily' to the home. . . . The State cannot 'assume the worst when people go to worship but assume the best when people go to work.' Roberts v. Neace, 958 F. 3d 409, 414 (CA6 2020) (per curiam). And fourth, although California officials changed the challenged policy shortly after this application was filed, the previous restrictions remain in place until April 15th, and officials with a track record of 'moving the goalposts' retain authority to reinstate those heightened restrictions at any time. . . .

"Applicants are likely to succeed on the merits of their free exercise claim; they are irreparably harmed by the loss of free exercise rights 'for even minimal periods of time'; and the State has not shown that 'public health would be imperiled' by employing less restrictive measures. *Roman Catholic Diocese*, ... Accordingly, applicants are entitled to an injunction pending appeal.

"This is the fifth time the Court has summarily rejected the Ninth Circuit's analysis of California's COVID restrictions on religious exercise. . . . It is unsurprising that such litigants are entitled to relief. California's Blueprint System contains myriad exceptions and accommodations for comparable activities, thus requiring the application of strict scrutiny. . . ."

Chief Justice Roberts did not file an opinion but would have denied the application. Justice Kagan, joined by Justices Breyer and Sotomayor, dissented, writing in part:

". . . California limits religious gatherings in homes to three households. If the State also limits all secular gatherings in homes to three households, it has complied with the First Amendment. And the State does exactly that: It has adopted a blanket restriction on at-home gatherings of all kinds, religious and secular alike. California need not, as the per curiam insists, treat at-home religious gatherings the same as hardware stores and hair salons—and thus unlike at-home secular gatherings, the obvious comparator here. . . . [T]he law does not require that the State equally treat apples and watermelons.

"And even supposing a court should cast so expansive a comparative net, the per curiam's analysis . . . defies the factual record. . . . [As the Ninth Circuit majority explained,] those [public] activities do pose lesser risks for at least three reasons. First, 'when people gather in social settings, their interactions are likely to be longer than they would be in a commercial setting,' with participants 'more likely to be involved in prolonged conversations.' . . . Second, 'private houses are typically smaller and less ventilated than commercial establishments.' . . . And third, 'social distancing and mask-wearing are less likely in private settings and enforcement is more difficult.' . . . These are not the mere musings of two appellate judges: The district court found each of these facts based on the uncontested testimony of California's public-health experts. . . ."

Page 1886. Add after Masterpiece Cakeshop, Ltd. v. Colorado Civil Rights Commission:

Fulton v. City of Philadelphia
593 U.S. ___, 141 S.Ct. 1868, ___ L.Ed.2d ___ (2021).

■ CHIEF JUSTICE ROBERTS delivered the opinion of the Court.

[The City's Department of Human Services assumes custody of children who cannot remain in their homes and pursues foster care placements for them through standard annual contracts with state-licensed private foster agencies like Catholic Social Services (CSS). Under Pennsylvania law, foster agencies must conduct a home study review of prospective foster parents and decide whether to "approve, disapprove or provisionally approve the foster family." When the Department seeks a referral, the agencies "report whether any of their certified families are available, and the Department places the child with what it regards as the most suitable family."]

. . . Because [CSS] understands the certification of prospective foster families to be an endorsement of their relationships, it will not certify unmarried couples—regardless of their sexual orientation—or same-sex married couples. CSS does not object to certifying gay or lesbian individuals as single foster parents or to placing gay and lesbian children. No same-sex couple has ever sought certification from CSS. If one did, CSS would direct the couple to one of the more than 20 other agencies in the City, all of which currently certify same-sex couples. For over 50 years, CSS successfully contracted with the City to provide foster care services while holding to these beliefs.

But . . . in 2018[, after a newspaper report] in which a spokesman for the Archdiocese of Philadelphia stated that CSS would not be able to consider prospective foster parents in same-sex marriages[, the] City Council called for an investigation, . . . [t]he Philadelphia Commission on Human Relations launched an inquiry[, a]nd the Commissioner of the Department [met] with the leadership of CSS. . . . Immediately after the meeting, the Department informed CSS that it would no longer refer children to the agency. The City later explained that the refusal of CSS to certify same-sex couples violated a non-discrimination provision in its contract with the City as well as the non-discrimination requirements of the citywide Fair Practices Ordinance. The City stated that it would not enter a full foster care contract with CSS in the future unless the agency agreed to certify same-sex couples.

CSS . . . [sued] the City, the Department, and the Commission[,] . . . alleg[ing] that the referral freeze violated the Free Exercise and Free Speech Clauses of the First Amendment. . . .

The District Court denied preliminary relief. It concluded that the contractual non-discrimination requirement and the Fair Practices Ordinance were neutral and generally applicable under Employment Division, Department of Human Resources of Oregon v. Smith, 494 U. S. 872 (1990), and that the free exercise claim was therefore unlikely to succeed.

The . . . Third Circuit affirmed. . . .

CSS . . . challenged the Third Circuit's determination that the City's actions were permissible under *Smith* and also asked this Court to reconsider that precedent.

. . .

II

A

. . . [I]t is plain that the City's actions have burdened CSS's religious exercise by putting it to the choice of curtailing its mission or approving relationships inconsistent with its beliefs. The City disagrees. In its view, certification reflects only that foster parents satisfy the statutory criteria, not that the agency endorses their relationships. But CSS believes that certification is tantamount to endorsement. And "religious beliefs need not be acceptable, logical, consistent, or comprehensible to others in order to merit First Amendment protection." Thomas v. Review Bd. of Ind. Employment Security Div., 450 U. S. 707, 714 (1981). . . .

Smith held that laws incidentally burdening religion are ordinarily not subject to strict scrutiny under the Free Exercise Clause so long as they are neutral and generally applicable. . . . CSS urges us to overrule *Smith*, and the concurrences in the judgment argue in favor of doing so. . . . But we need not revisit that decision here. This case falls outside *Smith* because the City has burdened the religious exercise of CSS through policies that do not meet the requirement of being neutral and generally applicable. . . .

Government fails to act neutrally when it proceeds in a manner intolerant of religious beliefs or restricts practices because of their religious nature. See Masterpiece Cakeshop, Ltd. v. Colorado Civil Rights Comm'n, . . .); *Lukumi*, ... CSS points to evidence in the record that it believes demonstrates that the City has transgressed this neutrality standard, but we find it more straightforward to resolve this case under the rubric of general applicability.

A law is not generally applicable if it "invite[s]" the government to consider the particular reasons for a person's conduct by providing " 'a mechanism for individualized exemptions.' " *Smith*, ...[;] Sherbert v. Verner, 374 U. S. 398 (1963)[. . . .]

. . . *Smith* [held] that "where the State has in place a system of individual exemptions, it may not refuse to extend that system to cases of 'religious hardship' without compelling reason." . . .

A law also lacks general applicability if it prohibits religious conduct while permitting secular conduct that undermines the government's asserted interests in a similar way. . . . Church of Lukumi Babalu Aye, Inc. v. Hialeah . . . .

B

. . . [S]ection 3.21 of [the City's] standard foster care contract . . . is not generally applicable as required by *Smith*. . . . [It] specifies in pertinent part:

> **Rejection of Referral**. Provider shall not reject a child or family including, but not limited to, . . . prospective foster or adoptive parents, for Services based upon . . . their . . . sexual orientation . . . unless an exception is granted by the Commissioner or the Commissioner's designee, in his/her sole discretion."

. . .

Like the good cause provision in *Sherbert*, section 3.21 incorporates a system of individual exemptions, made available in this case at the "sole discretion" of the Commissioner. The City has made clear that the Commissioner "has no intention of granting an exception" to CSS. . . . But the City "may not refuse to extend that [exemption] system to cases of 'religious hardship' without compelling reason." *Smith*, 494 U. S., at 884 . . . .

The City . . . argue[s] that governments should enjoy greater leeway under the Free Exercise Clause when setting rules for contractors than when regulating the general public. . . .

. . . We have never suggested that the government may discriminate against religion when acting in its managerial role. And *Smith* itself drew support for the neutral and generally applicable standard from cases involving internal government affairs. See 494 U. S., at 883–885, and n. 2 (citing Lyng v. Northwest Indian Cemetery Protective Assn., 485 U. S. 439 (1988) . . . . The City . . . accordingly ask[s] only that courts apply a more deferential approach in determining whether a policy is neutral and generally applicable in the contracting context. We find no need to resolve that narrow issue in this case. No matter the level of deference we extend to the City, the inclusion of a formal system of entirely discretionary exceptions in section 3.21 renders the contractual nondiscrimination requirement not generally applicable.

. . .

The City . . . add[s] that, notwithstanding the system of exceptions in section 3.21, a separate provision in the contract independently prohibits discrimination in the certification of foster parents. That provision, section 15.1, bars discrimination on the basis of sexual orientation, and it does not on its face allow for exceptions. . . . But state law makes clear that . . . an exception from section 3.21 also must govern the prohibition in section 15.1, lest the City's reservation of the authority to grant such an exception be a nullity. As a result, the contract as a whole contains no generally applicable non-discrimination requirement.

Finally, the City . . . contend[s] that the availability of exceptions under section 3.21 is irrelevant because the Commissioner has never granted one. That misapprehends the issue. The creation of a formal mechanism for granting exceptions renders a policy not generally applicable, regardless whether any exceptions have been given, because it "invite[s]" the government to decide which reasons for not complying with the policy are worthy of solicitude, *Smith*, 494 U. S., at 884—here, at the Commissioner's "sole discretion."

. . .

C

. . . [T]he City [also] argues that CSS's refusal to certify same-sex couples constitutes an "Unlawful Public Accommodations Practice[ ]" in violation of the Fair Practices Ordinance. That ordinance forbids "deny[ing] or interfer[ing] with the public accommodations opportunities of an individual or otherwise discriminat[ing] based on his or her race, ethnicity, color, sex, sexual orientation, . . . disability, marital status, familial status," or several other protected categories. Phila. Code § 9–1106(1) (2016). The City contends that foster care agencies are public accommodations and therefore forbidden from discriminating on the basis of sexual orientation when certifying foster parents.

. . . We conclude that . . . foster care agencies do not act as public accommodations in performing certifications.

The ordinance defines a public accommodation in relevant part as "[a]ny place, provider or public conveyance, whether licensed or not, which solicits or accepts the patronage or trade of the public or whose goods, services, facilities, privileges, advantages or accommodations are extended, offered, sold, or otherwise made available to the public." § 9–1102(1)(w). Certification is not "made available to the public" in the usual sense of the words. . . . A Pennsylvania antidiscrimination statute similarly defines a public accommodation as an accommodation that is "open to, accepts or solicits the patronage of the general public." . . . The "common theme" is that a public accommodation must "provide a benefit to the general public allowing individual members of the general public to avail themselves of that benefit if they so desire." Blizzard v. Floyd, 149 Pa. Commw. 503, 506, 613 A. 2d 619, 621 (1992).

Certification as a foster parent, by contrast, is not readily accessible to the public. It involves a customized and selective assessment that bears little resemblance to staying in a hotel, eating at a restaurant, or riding a bus. The process takes three to six months. Applicants must pass background checks and a medical exam. Foster agencies are required to conduct an intensive home study during which they evaluate, among other things, applicants' "mental and emotional adjustment," "community ties with family, friends, and neighbors," and "[e]xisting family relationships, attitudes and expectations regarding the applicant's own children and parent/child relationships." 55 Pa. Code § 3700.64. Such inquiries would raise eyebrows at the local bus station. . . . [T]he one-size-fits-all public accommodations model is a poor match for the foster care system.

[Justice Gorsuch's] concurrence adopts the City's argument, seeing no incongruity in deeming a private religious foster agency a public accommodation. We respectfully disagree . . . . The District Court did not take into account the uniquely selective nature of the certification process, which must inform the applicability of the ordinance. We agree with CSS's position . . . that its "foster services do not constitute a 'public accommodation' under the City's Fair Practices Ordinance, and therefore it is not bound by that ordinance." . . . We therefore have no need to assess whether the ordinance is generally applicable.

III

The contractual non-discrimination requirement imposes a burden on CSS's religious exercise and does not qualify as generally applicable. . . . Because the City's actions are therefore examined under the strictest scrutiny regardless of *Smith*, we have no occasion to reconsider that decision here.

. . . [S]o long as the government can achieve its interests in a manner that does not burden religion, it must do so.

The City asserts that its non-discrimination policies serve three compelling interests: maximizing the number of foster parents, protecting the City from liability, and ensuring equal treatment of prospective foster parents and foster children. . . . The question . . . is not whether the City has a compelling interest in enforcing its non-discrimination policies generally, but whether it has such an interest in denying an exception to CSS.

Once properly narrowed, the City's asserted interests are insufficient. Maximizing the number of foster families and minimizing liability are important goals, but the City fails to show that granting CSS an exception will put those goals at risk. If anything, including CSS in the program seems likely to increase, not reduce, the number of available foster parents. As for liability, the City offers only speculation that it might be sued over CSS's certification practices. Such speculation is insufficient to satisfy strict scrutiny, . . . particularly because the authority to certify foster families is delegated to agencies by the State, not the City . . . .

That leaves the interest of the City in the equal treatment of prospective foster parents and foster children. We do not doubt that this interest is a weighty one, for "[o]ur society has come to the recognition that gay persons and gay couples cannot be treated as social outcasts or as inferior in dignity and worth." *Masterpiece Cakeshop*, ... On the facts of this case, however, this interest cannot justify denying CSS an exception for its religious exercise. The creation of a system of exceptions under the contract undermines the City's contention that its nondiscrimination policies can brook no departures. See *Lukumi*, 508 U. S., at 546–547. The City offers no compelling reason why it has a particular interest in denying an exception to CSS while making them available to others.

* * *

. . . CSS seeks only an accommodation that will allow it to continue serving the children of Philadelphia in a manner consistent with its religious beliefs; it does not seek to impose those beliefs on anyone else. The refusal of Philadelphia to contract with CSS for the provision of foster care services unless it agrees to certify same-sex couples as foster parents cannot survive strict scrutiny . . . .

In view of our conclusion that the actions of the City violate the Free Exercise Clause, we need not consider whether they also violate the Free Speech Clause.

The judgment . . . is reversed, and the case is remanded . . . .

■ JUSTICE BARRETT, with whom JUSTICE KAVANAUGH joins, and with whom JUSTICE BREYER joins as to all but the first paragraph, concurring.

. . . Petitioners, their *amici*, scholars, and Justices of this Court have made serious arguments that *Smith* ought to be overruled. While history looms large in this debate, I find the historical record more silent than supportive on the question whether the founding generation understood the First Amendment to require religious exemptions from generally applicable laws in at least some circumstances. In my view, the textual and structural arguments against *Smith* are more compelling. As a matter of text and structure, it is difficult to see why the Free Exercise Clause—lone among the First Amendment freedoms—offers nothing more than protection from discrimination.

Yet what should replace *Smith*? The prevailing assumption seems to be that strict scrutiny would apply whenever a neutral and generally applicable law burdens religious exercise. But I am skeptical about swapping *Smith*'s categorical antidiscrimination approach for an equally categorical strict scrutiny regime, particularly when this Court's resolution of conflicts between generally applicable laws and other First Amendment rights—like speech and assembly—has been much more nuanced. There would be a number of issues to work through if *Smith* were overruled. To name a few: Should entities like Catholic Social Services—which is an arm of the Catholic Church—be treated differently than individuals? Cf. Hosanna-Tabor Evangelical Lutheran Church and School v. EEOC, 565 U. S. 171 (2012). Should there be a distinction between indirect and direct burdens on religious exercise? Cf. Braunfeld v. Brown, 366 U. S. 599, 606–607 (1961) (plurality opinion). What forms of scrutiny should apply? Compare Sherbert v. Verner, 374 U. S. 398, 403 (1963) (assessing whether government's interest is " 'compelling' "), with Gillette v. United States, 401 U. S. 437, 462 (1971) (assessing whether government's interest is "substantial"). And if the answer is strict scrutiny, would pre-*Smith* cases rejecting free exercise challenges to garden-variety laws come out the same way? See *Smith*, 494 U. S., at 888–889.

We need not wrestle with these questions in this case, though, because the same standard applies regardless whether *Smith* stays or goes. A longstanding tenet of our free exercise jurisprudence—one that both pre-dates and survives *Smith*—is that a law burdening religious exercise must satisfy strict scrutiny if it gives government officials discretion to grant individualized exemptions. . . . And all nine Justices agree that the City cannot satisfy strict scrutiny. I therefore see no reason to decide in this case whether Smith should be overruled, much less what should replace it. I join the Court's opinion in full.

■ JUSTICE ALITO, with whom JUSTICE THOMAS and JUSTICE GORSUCH join, concurring in the judgment.

. . .

Regrettably, the Court declines to [confront whether *Smith* should be reconsidered.] Instead, it reverses based on what appears to be a superfluous (and likely to be short-lived) feature of the City's standard annual contract with foster care agencies. *Smith*'s holding about categorical rules does not apply if a rule permits individualized exemptions, 494 U. S., at 884, and the majority seizes on the presence in the City's standard contract of language giving a City official the power to grant exemptions. The City tells us that it has never granted such an exemption and has no intention of handing one to CSS, . . . but the majority reverses . . . because the contract supposedly confers that never-used power.

This decision might as well be written on the dissolving paper sold in magic shops. The City has been adamant about pressuring CSS to give in, and if the City wants to get around today's decision, it can simply eliminate the never-used exemption power. If it does that, then, voilà, today's decision will vanish—and the parties will be back where they started. The City will claim that it is protected by *Smith*; CSS will argue that *Smith* should be overruled; the lower courts, bound by *Smith*, will reject that argument; and CSS will file a new petition in this Court challenging *Smith*. What is the point of going around in this circle?

. . .

We should reconsider *Smith* without further delay. The correct interpretation of the Free Exercise Clause is a question of great importance, and *Smith*'s interpretation is hard to defend. It can't be squared with the ordinary meaning of the text of the Free Exercise Clause or with the prevalent understanding of the scope of the free-exercise right at the time of the First Amendment's adoption. It swept aside decades of established precedent, and it has not aged well. Its interpretation has been undermined by subsequent scholarship on the original meaning of the Free Exercise Clause. Contrary to what many initially expected, *Smith* has not provided a clear-cut rule that is easy to apply, and experience has disproved the *Smith* majority's fear that retention of the Court's prior free-exercise jurisprudence would lead to "anarchy." 494 U. S., at 888.

II

A

. . .

The test distilled from *Sherbert*—that a law that imposes a substantial burden on the exercise of religion must be narrowly tailored to serve a compelling interest—was the governing rule for the next 37 years. Applying that test, the Court sometimes vindicated free-exercise claims. . . .

. . .

Other cases applied *Sherbert* but found no violation. . . .

B

This is where our case law stood when *Smith* reached the Court. . . .

. . .

. . . [W]ithout briefing or argument on whether *Sherbert* should be cast aside, the Court adopted what it seems to have thought was a clear-cut test that would be easy to apply: A "generally applicable and otherwise valid" rule does not violate the Free Exercise Clause "if prohibiting the exercise of religion . . . is not [its] object . . . but merely the incidental effect of" its operation. 494 U. S., at 878. Other than cases involving rules that target religious conduct, the *Sherbert* test was held to apply to only two narrow categories of cases: (1) those involving the award of unemployment benefits or other schemes allowing individualized exemptions and (2) so-called "hybrid rights" cases. See 494 U. S., at 881–884.

To clear the way for this new regime, the majority was willing to take liberties. Paying little attention to the terms of the Free Exercise Clause, it was satisfied that its interpretation represented a "permissible" reading of the text, *Smith*, 494 U. S., at 878, and it did not even stop to explain why that was so. The majority made no effort to ascertain the original understanding of the free-exercise right, and it limited past precedents on grounds never previously suggested. *Sherbert*, *Thomas*, and *Hobbie* were placed in a special category because they concerned the award of unemployment compensation, *Smith*, 494 U. S., at 883, and *Yoder* was distinguished on the ground that it involved both a free-exercise claim and a parental-rights claim, *Smith*, 494 U. S., at 881. Not only did these distinctions lack support in prior case law, the issue in *Smith* itself could easily be viewed as falling into both of these special categories. After all, it involved claims for unemployment benefits, and members of the Native American Church who ingest peyote as part of a religious ceremony are surely engaging in expressive conduct that falls within the scope of the Free Speech Clause. See, e.g., Texas v. Johnson, 491 U. S. 397, 404 (1989).

None of these obstacles stopped the *Smith* majority from adopting its new rule and displacing decades of precedent. . . .

. . .

Smith's impact was quickly felt, and Congress . . . attempted to restore the *Sherbert* test. . . . [T]he Religious Freedom Restoration Act (RFRA), passed in the House without dissent, was approved in the Senate by a vote of 97 to 3, and was enthusiastically signed into law by President Clinton. . . . And when this Court later held in *City of Boerne*, 521 U. S. 507, that Congress lacked the power under the 14th Amendment to impose these rules on the States, Congress responded by enacting the Religious Land Use and Institutionalized Persons Act (RLUIPA) under its spending power and its power to regulate interstate commerce. . . . RLUIPA imposed the same rules as RFRA on land use and prison regulations. . . . RLUIPA passed both Houses of Congress without a single negative vote and, like RFRA, was signed by President Clinton. . . .

RFRA and RLUIPA have restored part of the protection that *Smith* withdrew, but they are both limited in scope and can be weakened or repealed by Congress at any time. They are no substitute for a proper interpretation of the Free Exercise Clause.

III

A

That project must begin with the constitutional text. . . .

. . .

B

. . . [W]e can . . . focus on . . . the term "prohibiting" and the phrase "the free exercise of religion."

. . . [T]he ordinary meaning of "prohibiting the free exercise of religion" was (and still is) forbidding or hindering unrestrained religious practices or worship. That straightforward understanding is a far cry from the interpretation adopted in *Smith*. It certainly does not suggest a distinction between laws that are generally applicable and laws that are targeted.

As interpreted in *Smith*, the Clause is essentially an antidiscrimination provision: It means that the Federal Government and the States cannot restrict conduct that constitutes a religious practice for some people unless it imposes the same restriction on everyone else who engages in the same conduct. *Smith* made no real attempt to square that equal-treatment interpretation with the ordinary meaning of the Free Exercise Clause's language, and it is hard to see how that could be done. The key point for present purposes is that the text of the Free Exercise Clause gives a specific group of people (those who wish to engage in the "exercise of religion") the right to do so without hindrance. The language of the Clause does not tie this right to the treatment of persons not in this group.

. . .

C

. . .

[To the possible argument that e]ven if a law prohibits conduct that constitutes an essential religious practice, it cannot be said to "prohibit" the free exercise of religion unless that was the lawmakers' specific object[, Justice Alito responded as follows:]

This is a hair-splitting interpretation. It certainly does not represent the "normal and ordinary" meaning of the Free Exercise Clause's terms. . . . Consider how it would play out if applied to some . . . hypothetical laws . . . . A law categorically banning all wine would not "prohibit" the celebration of a Catholic Mass? A law categorically forbidding the slaughter of a conscious animal would not "prohibit" kosher and halal slaughterhouses? A rule categorically banning any head covering in a courtroom would not "prohibit" appearances by orthodox Jewish men, Sikh men, and Muslim women who wear hijabs? It is no wonder that *Smith*'s many defenders have almost uniformly foregone this argument.

D

Not only is it difficult to square Smith's interpretation with the terms of the Free Exercise Clause, the absence of any language referring to equal treatment is striking. . . .

. . . Other constitutional provisions contain non-discrimination language. For example, Art. I, § 9, cl. 6, provides that "[n]o Preference shall be given by any Regulation of Commerce or Revenue to the Ports of one State over those of another." Under Art. IV, § 2, cl. 1, "[t]he Citizens of each State shall be entitled to all Privileges and Immunities of Citizens in the several States." Article V provides that "no State, without its Consent, shall be deprived of its equal Suffrage in the Senate." Language mandating equal treatment of one sort or another also appeared in the religious liberty provisions of colonial charters and state constitutions. But Congress eschewed those models. The contrast between these readily available anti-discrimination models and the language that appears in the First Amendment speaks volumes.

IV

A

While we presume that the words of the Constitution carry their ordinary and normal meaning, we cannot disregard the possibility that some of the terms in the Free Exercise Clause had a special meaning that was well understood at the time. . . .

. . . [W]e must ask whether the Free Exercise Clause protects a right that was known at the time of adoption to have defined dimensions. But in doing so, we must keep in mind that there is a presumption that the words of the Constitution are to be interpreted in accordance with their "normal and ordinary" sense. . . .

B

1

What was the free-exercise right understood to mean when the Bill of Rights was ratified? And in particular, was it clearly understood that the right simply required equal treatment for religious and secular conduct? When *Smith* was decided, scholars had not devoted much attention to the original meaning of the Free Exercise Clause, and the parties' briefs ignored this issue, as did the opinion of the Court. Since then, however, the historical record has been plumbed in detail, and we are now in a good position to examine how the free-exercise right was understood when the First Amendment was adopted.

By that date, the right to religious liberty already had a long, rich, and complex history in this country. . . . [B]y 1789, every State except Connecticut had a constitutional provision protecting religious liberty. . . . In all of those State Constitutions, freedom of religion enjoyed broad protection, and the right "was universally said to be an unalienable right." . . .

2

. . .

When we look at these provisions, we see one predominant model. This model extends broad protection for religious liberty but expressly provides that the right does not protect conduct that would endanger "the public peace" or "safety."

. . .

3

The model favored by Congress and the state legislatures—providing broad protection for the free exercise of religion except where public "peace" or "safety" would be endangered—is antithetical to *Smith*. If, as *Smith* held, the free-exercise right does not require any religious exemptions from generally applicable laws, it is not easy to imagine situations in which a public-peace-or-safety carveout would be necessary. Legislatures enact generally applicable laws to protect public peace and safety. If those laws are thought to be sufficient to address a particular type of conduct when engaged in for a secular purpose, why wouldn't they also be sufficient to address the same type of conduct when carried out for a religious reason?

Smith's defenders have no good answer. . . .

. . .

. . . [T]he ordinary meaning of offenses that threaten public peace or safety must be stretched beyond the breaking point to encompass all violations of any law.

C

That the free-exercise right included the right to certain religious exemptions is strongly supported by the practice of the Colonies and States. When there were important clashes between generally applicable laws and the religious practices of particular groups, colonial and state legislatures were willing to grant exemptions—even when the generally applicable laws served critical state interests.

[Justice Alito cited as examples oath exemptions for religious objectors, exemptions from military conscription, colonial exemptions from special taxes for supporting ministers of established churches, and other exemptions.]

In an effort to dismiss the significance of these legislative exemptions, it has been argued that they show only what the Constitution permits, not what it requires. *City of Boerne*, 521 U. S., at 541 (opinion of Scalia, J.). But legislatures provided those accommodations before the concept of judicial review took hold, and their actions are therefore strong evidence of the founding era's understanding of the free-exercise right. . . .

D

Defenders of *Smith* have advanced historical arguments of their own, but they are unconvincing, and in any event, plainly insufficient to overcome the ordinary meaning of the constitutional text.

. . .

. . . Indeed, the case against *Smith* is very convincing.

V

. . .

In assessing whether to overrule a past decision that appears to be incorrect, we have considered a variety of factors, and four of those weigh strongly against *Smith*: its reasoning; its consistency with other decisions; the workability of the rule that it established; and developments since the decision was handed down. . . . No relevant factor, including reliance, weighs in *Smith*'s favor.

A

Smith's reasoning. As explained in detail above, *Smith* is a methodological outlier. . . .

. . .

[Among other deficiencies,] there is the problem that the hybrid-rights exception would largely swallow up *Smith*'s general rule. A great many claims for religious exemptions can easily be understood as hybrid free-exercise/free-speech claims. Take the claim in *Smith* itself. To members of the Native American Church, the ingestion of peyote during a religious ceremony is a sacrament. When Smith and Black participated in this sacrament, weren't they engaging in a form of expressive conduct? Their ingestion of peyote "communicate[d], in a rather dramatic way, [their] faith in the tenets of the Native American Church," and the State's prohibition of that practice "interfered with their ability to communicate this message" in violation of the Free Speech Clause. McConnell, Free Exercise Revisionism 1122. And, "if a hybrid claim is one in which a litigant would actually obtain an exemption from a formally neutral, generally applicable law under another constitutional provision, then there would have been no reason for the Court in [the so-called] hybrid cases to have mentioned the Free Exercise Clause at all." *Lukumi*, 508 U. S., at 566–567 (opinion of Souter, J.) . . . . It is telling that this Court has never once accepted a "hybrid rights" claim in the more than three decades since *Smith*.

In addition to all these maneuvers—creating special categories for unemployment compensation cases, cases involving individualized exemptions, and hybrid-rights cases—*Smith* ignored the multiple occasions when the Court had directly repudiated the very rule that Smith adopted.

Smith's rough treatment of prior decisions diminishes its own status as a precedent.

B

Consistency with other precedents. . . . *Smith* did not overrule *Sherbert* or any of the other cases that built on *Sherbert* from 1963 to 1990, and . . . *Smith* is tough to harmonize with those precedents.

The same is true about more recent decisions [like] Hosanna-Tabor Evangelical Lutheran Church and School v. EEOC, 565 U. S. 171 (2012), [and] Our Lady of Guadalupe School v. Morrissey-Berru, 591 U. S. ___, ___–___ (2020) . . . .

There is also tension between *Smith* and our opinion in Masterpiece Cakeshop, Ltd. v. Colorado Civil Rights Comm'n, ... In that case, we observed that "[w]hen it comes to weddings, it can be assumed that a member of the clergy who objects to gay marriage on moral and religious grounds could not be compelled to perform the ceremony without denial of his or her right to the free exercise of religion." . . . The clear import of this observation is that such a member of the clergy would be entitled to a religious exemption from a state law restricting the authority to perform a state-recognized marriage to individuals who are willing to officiate both opposite-sex and same-sex weddings.

. . .

C

Workability. One of *Smith*'s supposed virtues was ease of application, but . . . at least four serious problems have arisen and continue to plague courts when called upon to apply *Smith*.

1

. . . The "hybrid rights" exception, which was essential to distinguish *Yoder*, has baffled the lower courts. . . .

. . .

It is rare to encounter a holding of this Court that has so thoroughly stymied or elicited such open derision from the Courts of Appeals.

2

Rules that "target" religion. Post-*Smith* cases have also struggled with the task of determining whether a purportedly neutral rule "targets" religious exercise or has the restriction of religious exercise as its "object." . . .

. . .

Decisions of the lower courts on the issue of targeting remain in disarray. . . .

3

The nature and scope of exemptions. There is confusion about the meaning of *Smith*'s holding on exemptions from generally applicable laws. Some decisions apply this special rule if multiple secular exemptions are granted. . . . Others conclude that even one secular exemption is enough. . . . And still others have applied the rule where the law, although allowing no exemptions on its face, was widely unenforced in cases involving secular conduct. . . .

4

Identifying appropriate comparators. To determine whether a law provides equal treatment for secular and religious conduct, two steps are required. First, a court must identify the secular conduct with which the religious conduct is to be compared. Second, the court must determine whether the State's reasons for regulating the religious conduct apply with equal force to the secular conduct with which it is compared. See *Lukumi*, 508 U. S., at 543. In *Smith*, this inquiry undoubtedly seemed straightforward: The secular conduct and the religious conduct prohibited by the Oregon criminal statute were identical. But things are not always that simple.

Cases involving rules designed to slow the spread of COVID-19 have driven that point home. State and local rules adopted for this purpose have typically imposed different restrictions for different categories of activities. Sometimes religious services have been placed in a category with certain secular activities, and sometimes religious services have been given a separate category of their own. To determine whether COVID-19 rules provided neutral treatment for religious and secular conduct, it has been necessary to compare the restrictions on religious services with the restrictions on secular activities that present a comparable risk of spreading the virus, and identifying the secular activities that should be used for comparison has been hotly contested.

. . .

Smith seemed to offer a relatively simple and clear-cut rule that would be easy to apply. Experience has shown otherwise.

D

Subsequent developments. . . . The *Smith* majority thought that adherence to *Sherbert* would invite "anarchy," but experience has shown that this fear was not well founded. Both RFRA and RLUIPA impose essentially the same requirements as *Sherbert*, and we have observed that the courts are well "up to the task" of applying that test. Gonzales v. O Centro Espírita Beneficente União do Vegetal, 546 U. S. 418, 436 (2006). . . .

Another significant development is the subsequent profusion of studies on the original meaning of the Free Exercise Clause. When *Smith* was decided, the available scholarship was thin, and the Court received no briefing on the subject. Since then, scholars have explored the subject in great depth.

. . .

E

. . . Reliance is often the strongest factor favoring the retention of a challenged precedent, but no strong reliance interests are cited in any of the numerous briefs urging us to preserve *Smith*. . . .

. . .

Smith was wrongly decided. As long as it remains on the books, it threatens a fundamental freedom. And while precedent should not lightly be cast aside, the Court's error in *Smith* should now be corrected.

VI

A

If *Smith* is overruled, what legal standard should be applied in this case? . . . A law that imposes a substantial burden on religious exercise can be sustained only if it is narrowly tailored to serve a compelling government interest.

Whether this test should be rephrased or supplemented with specific rules is a question that need not be resolved here because Philadelphia's ouster of CSS from foster care work simply does not further any interest that can properly be protected in this case. . . . CSS's policy has not hindered any same-sex couples from becoming foster parents, and there is no threat that it will do so in the future.

CSS's policy has only one effect: It expresses the idea that same-sex couples should not be foster parents because only a man and a woman should marry. Many people today find this idea not only objectionable but hurtful. Nevertheless, protecting against this form of harm is not an interest that can justify the abridgment of First Amendment rights.

We have covered this ground repeatedly in free speech cases. In an open, pluralistic, self-governing society, the expression of an idea cannot be suppressed simply because some find it offensive, insulting, or even wounding. . . .

The same fundamental principle applies to religious practices that give offense. The preservation of religious freedom depends on that principle. Many core religious beliefs are perceived as hateful by members of other religions or nonbelievers. . . .

Suppressing speech—or religious practice—simply because it expresses an idea that some find hurtful is a zero-sum game. While CSS's ideas about marriage are likely to be objectionable to same-sex couples, lumping those who hold traditional beliefs about marriage together with racial bigots is insulting to those who retain such beliefs. . . .

. . .

After receiving more than 2,500 pages of briefing and after more than a half-year of post-argument cogitation, the Court has emitted a wisp of a decision that leaves religious liberty in a confused and vulnerable state. Those who count on this Court to stand up for the First Amendment have every right to be disappointed—as am I.

■ JUSTICE GORSUCH, with whom JUSTICE THOMAS and JUSTICE ALITO join, concurring in the judgment.

[Justice Gorsuch's opinion is sharply critical of the majority's interpretation of the City's contract provisions, the City's Fair Practices Ordinance, and state law, as embodying policies that are not "generally applicable," thereby avoiding the need to confront directly whether *Smith* should be overruled.]

. . . One way or another, the majority seems determined to declare there is no "need" or "reason" to revisit *Smith* today.

But tell that to CSS. Its litigation has already lasted years—and today's (ir)resolution promises more of the same. Had we followed the path Justice Alito outlines—holding that the City's rules cannot avoid strict scrutiny even if they qualify as neutral and generally applicable—this case would end today. Instead, the majority's course guarantees that this litigation is only getting started. As the final arbiter of state law, the Pennsylvania Supreme Court can effectively overrule the majority's reading of the Commonwealth's public accommodations law. The City can revise its FPO to make even plainer still that its law does encompass foster services. Or with a flick of a pen, municipal lawyers may rewrite the City's contract to close the § 3.21 loophole.

Once any of that happens, CSS will find itself back where it started. The City has made clear that it will never tolerate CSS carrying out its foster-care mission in accordance with its sincerely held religious beliefs. . . . The City has expressed its determination to put CSS to a choice: Give up your sincerely held religious beliefs or give up serving foster children and families. . . .

. . .

We hardly need to "wrestle" today with every conceivable question that might follow from recognizing *Smith* was wrong. See (Barrett, J., concurring). To be sure, any time this Court turns from misguided precedent back toward the Constitution's original public meaning, challenging questions may arise across a large field of cases and controversies. But that's no excuse for refusing to apply the original public meaning in the dispute actually before us. Rather than adhere to *Smith* until we settle on some "grand unified theory" of the Free Exercise Clause for all future cases until the end of time, the Court should overrule it now, set us back on the correct course, and address each case as it comes.

. . .